Who I
Am In
Christ
Daily Devotionals

Who I Am In Christ Daily Devotionals

All Scripture quotations are taken from the New International Version of the Bible.

This book is based on a compilation of Biblical Truths to "Practice Believing" by Pastor Dick LaFountain. Used with permission.

Cover photo: Copyright Kevin Carden | Dreamstime.com
https://www.dreamstime.com/kevron2001_info

ISBN: 978-1-953759-56-6 (paperback)
ISBN: 978-1-953759-57-3 (eBook)

BOOK PUBLISHING

Revised Edition.

Printed in the United States of America.

We are giving away a powerful book for free titled "You Are Born To Win."

CLICK HERE to download for free.

To those who have the courage to believe for the impossible…

This book is for YOU!

Visit: www.corvillemcleish.com for more books and content that will help you on your faith journey.

To those whose sole desire is to become a full manifestation of God's intent when He said, "Let Us make man in Our image and likeness…"

Visit our youtube page @ God's Image Jamaica (God's Image Jamaica - YouTube)
Let us change the world one maturing soul at a time!

C. Orville McLeish

I Am Who God Says I Am Series
Book I

Who I
Am In
Christ
Daily Devotionals

101 Daily Devotionals And Declarations Of Faith

Declare. Believe. Receive. Become.

Do not judge yourself by your own thoughts, or the opinion of others. Be bold enough to believe what God says about you, even if everything and everyone else is trying to convince you otherwise.

You are who God says you are! Open your mouth and declare it: "I am who God says I am!"

Table of Contents

Acknowledgments

I want to thank David Jeremiah Roberts for his invaluable insights and contributions of various thoughts in this book.

I thank my wife, Nordia, for her continued love, support, and prayers.

Special thanks are due to Pastor Dick LaFountain for allowing me to use his work in completing this book.

I want to thank you for purchasing a copy of this book. I hope and pray that it will find its place at the side of your bed for daily inspirations and affirmations of faith in who you are in Christ Jesus. Be bold enough to declare these truths daily, even and especially in the face of fear and unbelief, and be ready for the transformation that will follow.

Foreword

by David Jeremiah Roberts

Who am I in Christ? Somehow we can never seem to get away from confronting and answering this question. This question seems appropriate to be asked in every generation of humanity that has come to the saving knowledge of Jesus Christ. There is no getting around it; we must answer this question in light of the revelations contained in scripture, and not from a modern world view. Our very walk as believers in Jesus the Messiah depends on how well we see ourselves in Him. We simply cannot advance in the Kingdom if we do not gain insights and understanding of who we are in Him, and the acceptance of what the Bible actually says about that subject.

My friend, C. Orville, has written an excellent book dealing with this fundamental issue from all sides. The answers to "Who I am in Christ" are in these chapters and on the pages in this book. I hope and trust that you will find your answer. "Who I am in Christ" will not only help you to answer this question, but it will also help to strengthen, solidify, and encourage your walk in the Kingdom, whether it has been a "long time walk" or a "new walk" in Christ.

My personal walk has been truly revolutionized as I have understood more and more about who I am in Christ. I am sure the same will happen to you. This book will help you to settle that question once and for all. This book will teach you that you are more than a conqueror, that you are Abba's (Father's) beloved, that you are seated in heavenly places, and more.

I fully endorse Who I Am in Christ Daily Devotionals, and I encourage you to get it for yourself, and also to bless another believer with a copy, and help that person to know who they are in Christ.

David Jeremiah Roberts

Author
propheticflow@hotmail.com
Kingston, Jamaica

Introduction

"Who Am I In Christ?" I could not answer this question the very first time I was asked by a minister. I had never really given it any thought prior to that pivotal moment in my life, and I had been "walking" with Christ for over a decade. A few things came to mind: I am redeemed, I am saved, I am well taken care of, I am protected. These are basic knowledge that we pick up along the way, but they don't necessarily provide a good answer to that very good question.

Most Christians are unable to answer this question. It's odd. We are told that there are over forty responses to this one question that speaks to our position in Christ. Finding ten off the top of your head could prove tough for the average Christian. Give it a try!

I needed to answer that question for myself. I gathered a small list of my positions in Christ, read it a few times, and then abandoned it. Months passed without thought. Then came my struggle with anxiety and fear. If we are familiar with those, we know they are more a state of mind than anything else; I was forced to take a second look at my mental health.

God sent another minister into my life who had a prophetic call on his life. He instructed me that, to overcome my anxieties, I had to rest my right hand on my forehead and declare that I had the mind of Christ, that I had power, love, and a sound mind.

This stirred my heart again to know who I was in Christ. I found a more extensive list of my positions in Christ and began reading them aloud every day, but God was pulling me in another direction. During one of my early morning meetings with God, I was instructed to write this book.

It was strange, as I thought I would need to grasp fully the answers I found to the question first, and maybe even experience some of them on a personal and supernatural level. Then again, God has His own unique way of doing things. I figured I should write this book so we can together grasp what it truly means to be "in Christ!"

As my knowledge increased as to who the Father is, I was encouraged to continue declaring these over my daily life. I invite you to do the same and begin to experience a transformation of your mind into the mind of Christ. You will begin to think your own thoughts after His, you will begin to hear Him speak back to you, and you will begin to experience the supernatural revelations of who He is, who you are, and what He is doing in this present age.

When Jesus came to earth, and died in our place, He restored the connection between heaven and earth that was severed by the fall. The Word declares that it is our 'iniquity' that separates us from God. So, if God removes our iniquity, then there is no more separation. The Kingdom of God is not a future state of being. It is a present reality. Jesus taught His disciples to pray by saying 'Thy Kingdom come on earth as it is in heaven." We say it, but we don't understand the gravity of our request.

For the kingdom of God is not a matter of talk but of power.
1 Corinthians 4:20

What keeps us from our true position in Christ is our ignorance. In our minds, we are still putting a partition between heaven and Earth, not realizing that what is happening in heaven, at this present moment, could be happening right here on Earth, "on Earth as it is in heaven."

Let us see if we can get back to the basics. The disciples and apostles knew who they were in Christ. In essence, the word "believer" takes on a whole new meaning when the Word declares that "signs and wonders follow those who believe." Apparently, this doesn't apply only to those who believe that Jesus lived, died, rose on the third day, and now sits at the right hand of God. I strongly believe that this applies to those who "believe" they are just like Christ in this present world.

> *This is how love is made complete among us so that we will*
> *have confidence on the day of judgment: In this world we*
> *are like Jesus.*
> *1 John 4:17*

It then behooves us to know, and believe, who we truly are in Christ.

This changed my life. I am confident it will do the same for you. This is not just a book. This is a journey, one that will take you from the ordinary to the supernatural.

Are you ready?

Day 1

I AM GOD'S POSSESSION

*And the LORD has declared this day that you are his
people, his treasured possession as he promised, and that you
are to keep all his commands.*
Deuteronomy 26:18

I am god's possession. If I "possess" something, then it belongs to me. Usually, a man will not lay claim to what another possesses, and even if he does, he knows that what he has belongs to someone else. We belong to God. It's a sobering thought. Who else can lay such a claim on the human race, but He who created us? He fashioned us in His likeness and image.

*Then God said, "Let us make mankind in our image, in
our likeness, so that they may rule over the fish in the sea and
the birds in the sky, over the livestock and all the wild
animals, and over all the creatures that move along the
ground."*
Genesis 1:26

We are a reflection of God. We cannot be likened to any other created being or thing. We are uniquely designed and created, fearfully and wonderfully made. Though we have been endowed with free will, we don't belong to ourselves. We belong to God. We are His possession, created for His purpose.

28

Today's Declaration:

I AM GOD'S POSSESSION

Day 2

I AM GOD'S CHILD

Yet to all who did receive him, to those who believed in his name, he gave the right to become children of God.
John 1:12

My earthly father died when I was thirty-five. I think myself more fortunate than others, but still it took a while to get over his death, natural though it was, simply because I was his child. Growing up, he ensured that we had shelter, food, clothes and opportunities for a proper education. As adults, he encouraged our choices, asked if we were okay, and helped to guide us where he could. We were his children.

The Word of God tells us that if our earthly father knows how to give good gifts and take care of his earthly children, how much more will our heavenly Father. To say we are His children should bring comfort and hope that we will always be taken care of. There is not a moment in any given day that our heavenly Father is not taking care of our needs, simply because we are His children.

Today's Declaration:

I AM GOD'S CHILD

Day 3

I AM GOD'S WORKMANSHIP

*For we are God's handiwork, created in Christ Jesus to do
good works, which God prepared in advance for us to do.*
Ephesians 2:10

We were designed and created by God. He formed us with His own hands.

But the original design was corrupted by our choice to sin. In that regard, our end would have been death, for the wages of sin is death. Instead, God chose to do a redesign through His Son, Jesus Christ.

Our perfection was restored through the sacrifice of His only begotten Son. Again, we became God's handiwork, as the first man was originally, formed and fashioned by His own hand. He will continue working on us until we are perfect and glorified.

Today's Declaration:

I AM GOD'S WORKMANSHIP

Day 4

I AM GOD'S FRIEND

*And the scripture was fulfilled that says, "Abraham
believed God, and it was credited to him as righteousness,"
and he was called God's friend.*
James 2:23

One of the songs our Church loves to sing is "I am a friend of God." We usually have a good time singing that song, but many of us don't stop to think about the words. What does it mean to be a friend of God? I imagine how difficult it must be for many to accept this biblical truth because we were brought up to think that God is not one of us. But didn't He become one of us, to save all of us?

Jesus had a close relationship with His disciples, many of whom critics thought were not worthy to be in the company of such a righteous man. He desires to have that same relationship with us. He laughed with them, ate with them, talked with them, and probably even played games with them. He was a friend of sinners. He is still our friend today.

Today's Declaration:

I AM GOD'S FRIEND

Day 5

I AM GOD'S TEMPLE

Don't you know that you yourselves are God's temple and
that God's Spirit dwells in your midst?
1 Corinthians 3:16

He was afraid and said, "How awesome is this place! This is
none other than the house of God; this is the gate of heaven."
Genesis 28:17

What we do in, and with, our bodies is important to God. It matters. The Word says we are to "present our bodies to God." This is our spiritual act of worship.

If we understand what salvation is all about, we know that because of sin we were dead. There is no life outside of Christ. For us to assume we can do as we please after He has pulled us out of death and into His abundant life is a little presumptuous. Christ paid for our sins so that He can live through us. Our eyes, ears, hands, feet, head, and body belong to Him. In Him we live, move, and have our being. In us dwells His Holy Spirit. When we move, He moves.

There was a time when God dwelled in a physical temple, a building made by the hands of men, but His desire has always been to dwell in the very temple He made with His hands. He lives in us. His presence is no longer in a structure or building, but we are carriers of God's divine presence. That is why wherever we are or wherever we go, there should be a difference. Where we are, God is.

Today's Declaration:

I AM GOD'S TEMPLE

Day 6

I AM GOD'S VESSEL

*If a man therefore purge himself from these, he shall be a
vessel unto honour, sanctified, and meet for the master's use,
and prepared unto every good work.*
2 Timothy 2:21

*But we have this treasure in earthen vessels, that the
excellency of the power may be of God, and not of us.*
2 Corinthians 4:7

When we think about vessels, we imagine a pot or bottle. Vessels are designed to hold or carry something. In this sense, we are carriers of God's presence. It's an enormous responsibility that we should not take lightly or for granted. If we are indeed vessels that carry the presence of God, then that should be what is poured out of us as well.

Another thing to note is that we would never pour oil and water into the same vessel. Some of us try to play a multi-purpose vessel for the world and Christ, but this mixture can only lead to disaster. Let us be carriers of the Kingdom of God so that He can live and flow through us.

Today's Declaration:

I AM GOD'S VESSEL

Day 7

I AM GOD'S CO-LABORER

For we are co-workers in God's service; you are God's field,
God's building.
1 Corinthians 3:9

God has always desired to partner with us in this world over which He made us governors. We were never intended to live and move outside of God. Man was to rule the Earth as God ruled the heavens. When sin entered our existence, a plan was already formulated that would redeem man. Jesus would come and die in our place. He was slain before the foundations of the world. In essence, this was God's plan to disempower sin and preserve the sinner.

Now God needs us even more to reach others with the message of salvation. We are His hands, feet, ears, and mouth in this world. Again, a partnership has been established, and we are God's channel – maybe even the only hope of reaching the lost. The harvest is ripe, but laborers were few back when those words were spoken. Today, God has millions of co-laborers, and you are one of them.

Today's Declaration:

I AM GOD'S CO-LABORER

Day 8

I AM GOD'S WITNESS

But you will receive power when the Holy Spirit comes on
you; and you will be my witnesses in Jerusalem, and in all
Judea and Samaria, and to the ends of the earth.
Acts 1:8

If we step outside our homes and take a one-mile walk, chances are we will pass many who are not saved. Measure the distance between where you live and where you go to school or work, and again we are talking about dozens or hundreds of unsaved people. Some of us go to church and expect that God will miraculously send everyone who is not saved to church to get saved. How unrealistic is that?

We are given the commission to go into all the world with the gospel. The gospel brings salvation to the lost. Those of us who are already saved received the gospel but how many of us received it in church?

God did not just send us; He also empowered us with His Holy Spirit. I understand the fear factor, the doubt factor, and all the reasons we push against actually being a witness, but if we are endowed with power from above, do we have an excuse? God made us witnesses of His power and enables and equips us to speak with power, authority, and wisdom to those who are yet to be born again. Read the text again! The Word did not say we will receive the Holy Spirit so we can jump around in church and talk in tongues.

The Word says we shall receive "power when the Holy Spirit comes on" us. This is the power to be a witness.

> *For the Spirit God gave us does not make us timid, but gives us power, love and self-discipline.*
> *2 Timothy 1:7*

Let us be bold and declare the gospel of our Lord Jesus Christ. There are billions still to hear it, and those in your circle may only get the opportunity to hear it from you. So, if not you, then who?

Today's Declaration:

I AM GOD'S WITNESS

Day 9

I AM GOD'S SOLDIER

*Join with me in suffering, like a good soldier of Christ
Jesus.*
2 Timothy 2:3

Paul was never a Roman soldier, and yet he gave several
illustrations and references to the soldiers of his time. For
example, "Put on the whole armor of God…"

He saw himself as a soldier of Jesus Christ. In essence, Christ
would be the Commander in Chief of this army. This is fitting when
we consider the words of Jesus: "If you love me, keep my
commandments." In other words, do what I say. Though God
desires an intimate and personal relationship with each of us, He
has also called us to become a part of his army in obedience to His
Word.

But let us examine the life of a soldier.

In a battle, there are many casualties. Soldiers march into battle
without fear, knowing that at any moment they could die. The fact
is, they are willing to die for the cause for which they fight. It is an
honor. To live or die is all the same to a soldier.

Jesus said those who try to save their life will lose it, but those
who are willing to give their lives for His sake will find it. Our
Commander in Chief takes no pleasure in fearful and disobedient
soldiers when He has declared us bold, strong, and worthy to fight

alongside Him. That sounds to me like a great honor. I am sure the apostle Paul agrees.

Today's Declaration:

I AM GOD'S SOLDIER

Day 10

I AM GOD'S AMBASSADOR

We are therefore Christ's ambassadors, as though God
were making his appeal through us. We implore you on
Christ's behalf: Be reconciled to God.
2 Corinthians 5:20

To be in Christ is a privileged position. We have been declared sons of God through Jesus Christ. We have been declared the righteousness of God through Jesus Christ. We are ambassadors. If we understand this term in a natural sense, we will see that we are direct representatives of Jesus Christ here on Earth. Can we fathom such a position?

Sinners are declared righteous and handed the keys to God's kingdom here on Earth. Whatever we loose on Earth is loosed in heaven and whatever we bind on Earth is bound in heaven. As Jesus is, so are we. So why the pity party? Why do we need somebody to feel sorry for us? The fullness of the Kingdom of God dwells in us, not partially, but complete in Christ.

In other words, everything that God wants to do on Earth, He intends to do through us.

"For in Christ all the fullness of the Deity lives in bodily form" (Colossians 2:9), and Christ lives in us through His Holy Spirit, "For God was pleased to have all his fullness dwell in him [Christ]" (Colossians 1:19), then in us.

Ephesians 3:16-19 - I pray that out of his glorious riches he may strengthen you with power through his Spirit in your inner being, so that Christ may dwell in your hearts through faith. And I pray that you, being rooted and established in love, may have power, together with all the Lord's holy people, to grasp how wide and long and high and deep is the love of Christ, and to know this love that surpasses knowledge—that you may be filled to the measure of all the fullness of God.

Today's Declaration:

I AM GOD'S AMBASSADOR

Day 11

I AM GOD'S BUILDING

For we are co-workers in God's service; you are God's
field, God's building.
1 Corinthians 3:9

As children, we often sang this song: "He's still working on me. To make me what I ought to be…" It is amazing that as children we have a much better understanding of what the Kingdom of God is all about. No wonder Jesus said that unless we become as little children, we cannot inherit His kingdom.

Sin did extensive damage to our temple (the body). God is restoring us to our original state. We cannot fix ourselves. Only Yahweh can restore this building to its former glory. It takes work, and it takes time, but the finished product will be a glorified body, just like Jesus.

For those God foreknew he also predestined to be
conformed to the image of his Son, that he might be the
firstborn among many brothers and sisters.
Romans 8:29

We were created in God's image and likeness. Sin distorted that image. We are daily being conformed back into the image of Christ, so we can again be a perfect reflection of our Father. This can be painful and uncomfortable at times, but it is very necessary.

Today's Declaration:

I AM GOD'S BUILDING

Day 12

I AM GOD'S MINISTER OR INSTRUMENT

Now get up and stand on your feet. I have appeared to you
to appoint you as a servant and as a witness of what you
have seen and will see of me.
Acts 26:16

If you point these things out to the brothers and sisters, you
will be a good minister of Christ Jesus, nourished on the
truths of the faith and of the good teaching that you have
followed.
1 Timothy 4:6

I learned something recently: that as independent as we think we are, we are just deceiving ourselves. God designed us to be dependent on other people and our environment. We need each other. We depend on our car to take us from place to place. We depend on our bosses or customers to pay us for work we do. We depend on cooks to make sure we have something to eat. We depend on farmers, chemists, mechanics, bank personnel, vendors, and more to help us in one way or another. Who can claim that they need no one? If it were indeed possible to disconnect ourselves from needing anyone, we would not have any clothes, shoes, soap, appliances, houses, cars…etc.

Likewise, we also depend on God whether we want to or not. He depends on us just the same. Without us, it would not be possible for God to reach others. What sinner do you know who is willing to listen to a voice in their heads telling them to be saved? None. We are empowered to speak the Word of God that produces conviction.

In this regard, we are ministers and instruments of God. He uses us for His glory. It was designed like this. If we think our value lies outside of God, we are mistaken.

Again, the natural helps us understand the spiritual. Think of a very expensive and beautiful keyboard. A musician obtains one of these and places it on a stand in the music corner of the church, and then he walks away and sits in the congregation. What good is an instrument absent the musician, despite its beauty and features? It has no value except to be admired, but is that its intended purpose? When the player applies himself to playing that keyboard, what transpires is something magical.

So it is with us, in the hands of God.

Today's Declaration:

I AM GOD'S MINISTER OR INSTRUMENT

Day 13

I AM GOD'S CHOSEN

*For he chose us in him before the creation of the world to be
holy and blameless in his sight. In love he predestined us
for adoption to sonship through Jesus Christ, in accordance
with his pleasure and will – to the praise of his glorious
grace, which he has freely given us in the One he loves.*
Ephesians 1:4-6

The word "chosen" suggests a careful and deliberate
selection. Here is what God says:

*Before I formed you in the womb I knew you, before you
were born I set you apart; I appointed you as a prophet to
the nations.*
Jeremiah 1:5

When a man ejaculates inside of a woman, there are 30-60
million sperms cells in that one batch. This means that there are at
least 30 million chances that the person born from that conception
would not have been you. I hope you got that. The sperm that
brought you into this world is one of the millions. If any other
sperm had touched that egg, you would not have been born.
Someone else, with a unique genetic code and fingerprint, would
have come in your place.

That only means you were divinely selected, and not just a random occurrence. God says before you were conceived, He knew you.

In the natural, we are subjected to time. God is not. In the spiritual, the past, present, and future are a present reality for God. He sees it all. He knows it all.

You may think you were an accident, but you are not. You may think you are the product of a nightmare, or a random act of pleasure seeking, but you are not. You are chosen and divinely appointed and supernaturally placed in your particular geographical location for this time.

God choose you out of millions of possibilities, and He calls you son or daughter. You are not a servant. We are the spiritual brothers and sisters of Jesus.

Today's Declaration:

I AM GOD'S CHOSEN

Day 14

I AM GOD'S BELOVED

*To all in Rome who are loved by God and called to be his
holy people: Grace and peace to you from God our Father
and from the Lord Jesus Christ.*
Romans 1:7

*But we ought always to thank God for you, brothers and
sisters loved by the Lord, because God chose you as
firstfruits to be saved through the sanctifying work of the
Spirit and through belief in the truth.*
2 Thessalonians 2:13

"Beloved" is defined as much loved, dearly loved, adored, favorite, and darling. Too often we think that when God looks at us, all He sees is our sin… and He often turns away. If this were true, Jesus would not have died on the cross for our sins, because He did that while looking at our sin for one final moment in history. Now God sees us in light of that sacrifice, which has rendered us God's darling. I say this proudly as a man of God as I grow in wisdom and understanding. I am precious in the eyes of the Lord, and so are you. Believing otherwise would be to deny the work of the cross.

God has put great value on us… sometimes even more than we place on ourselves. We often think we are not worthy, but Jesus has declared us worthy. We may believe that we are unclean, but Jesus has declared us clean. We may believe that we are just servants of God, but Jesus has declared us sons and daughters. Understand that we have been elevated to a position of royalty.

> *But you are a chosen people, a royal priesthood, a holy*
> *nation, God's special possession, that you may declare the*
> *praises of him who called you out of darkness into his*
> *wonderful light.*
> *1 Peter 2:9*

Today's Declaration:

I AM GOD'S BELOVED

Day 15

I AM GOD'S PRECIOUS JEWEL

"On the day when I act," says the Lord Almighty, "they will be my treasured possession. I will spare them, just as a father has compassion and spares his son who serves him."
Malachi 3:17

Many times, God was angry with the children of Israel. Though He declared them His prized possession, they would continually turn their backs on Him to serve idols, and follow their own way. What is remarkable is that despite what they did, the moment they called on Him for help, He was there ready to forgive and deliver.

We can identify with this kind of relationship. We are the apple of God's eye, a rare gem, a precious jewel. He pulled us out of the pit of sin, cleansed us, and transformed us.

But understand that He saw you as a precious jewel from the time you were messed up and tangled up in sin. He loves you that much. I can only surmise that the word "precious" suggest uniqueness. The Father takes joy in looking at us, caring for us, cleaning us up, and boasting about us. He said of Job, "Have you considered my servant?" He is saying the same thing about you.

It is hard for us to fathom God's thoughts towards us. In the eighth Psalm, David asked, "What is mankind that you are mindful of them, human beings that you care for them?" It is hard for us to understand His love when we mess up from time to time, but God knows your sin. He paid for it with His blood.

Practice repentance and never walk away from the presence of God. He desires to commune with you. In His eyes, you are precious.

Today's Declaration:

I AM GOD'S PRECIOUS JEWEL

Day 16

I AM GOD'S HERITAGE

*Neither as being lords over God's heritage, but being
examples to the flock.*
1 Peter 5:3

By now you must realize that, in the eyes of God, we are a valuable gem. All our Father has done, from the garden of Eden until this day, is for us. He has given everything for us. He sacrificed all for us. Everything the enemy took from us was restored to us by our Father. He blesses us, provides for us, feeds us, clothes us, and enables us to have a deep, intimate, and personal relationship with Him. We are tempted to believe that God doesn't see us, that somehow we are invisible to Him; this just proves how easily deceived we can be.

Think about it. This earth and all that it has to offer, the institution of marriage, our ability to procreate and have relations with each other, our talents and gifts, our ability to choose, feel, and create – God gave us all that. He created and gave us so much for our pleasure and enjoyment. Our problem is not that God doesn't bless us enough, but that we can be ungrateful for ninety-nine things we have received because of that one thing we did not get. We should be grateful at all times and contented with our lives because truthfully, God does treat us like royalty, and rightfully so: He has declared us worthy of such honor.

Today's Declaration:

I AM GOD'S HERITAGE

Day 17

I AM REDEEMED BY HIS BLOOD

*And they sang a new song: "You are worthy to take the
scroll and to open its seals, because you were slain, and
with your blood you purchased men for God from every
tribe and language and people and nation."*
Revelation 5:9

There is no remission of sin without the shedding of blood.
It is the blood of Jesus that covers a multitude of sins. We
learn this very early in Genesis after man fell from grace.
God provided coverings for them. This was symbolic of what Jesus
would do so many centuries later.

I sat on my verandah staring up at the sky one night, just
thinking about everything. The universe has no limits known to
man, and neither does God. Some theologians say that He lives in
the third heaven, which is somewhere beyond the heaven that
contains the stars, solar system, and so on. I'm thinking that is a
very long way off, so why would God leave there and come here to
such an insignificant speck like Earth and die for us? I was
overwhelmed at the thought, but also found solace and comfort in
knowing that from where God sits, the Earth is a dot, as any other
planet is just a dot to us from this perspective…but somehow He
loves us enough to reconnect with us, even after we told Him in no
uncertain terms that we can make our way without Him. God must
know something about us that we do not yet know to go to such
lengths to provide redemption for us all.

The bottom line is, the wages of sin is death – so either God died, or we would die. The choice has been made and we can now rest in full assurance and confidence in the finished work of the cross.

Today's Declaration:

I AM REDEEMED BY HIS BLOOD

Day 18

I AM SET FREE FROM SIN AND CONDEMNATION

Therefore, there is now no condemnation for those who are in Christ Jesus, because through Christ Jesus the law of the Spirit of life set me free from the law of sin and death.
Romans 8:1-2

As a child of God, I haven't always walked in total righteousness. I have been addicted to pornography, masturbation, and fornication. I struggled with these giants for years, not finding any lasting freedom and relief.

With this came guilt and condemnation. Even though I begged for God's forgiveness daily, I still felt extreme guilt and thought there was no way a perfect God could forgive me so many times for the same sin. It was a battle that I felt I would never win… but God is faithful.

When I finally learned that the battle was not mine to fight, I turned the wheel over to Him, and he has indeed delivered me from the sin – and the guilt. He did much more than that. I found freedom in Christ, and I don't even know when and how He did it, but one day I did a self-check and realized I no longer had any appetite for something that I once could not stop myself from doing.

Friends, believe me when I tell you that if God can deliver me from this, He can deliver anyone.

Today's Declaration:

I AM SET FREE FROM SIN AND CONDEMNATION

Day 19

I AM SET FREE FROM SATAN'S CONTROL

*For he has rescued us from the dominion of darkness and
brought us into the kingdom of the Son he loves.*
Colossians 1:13

The scriptures tell us that Jesus defeated principalities and powers and made a public spectacle of them. In other words, they were conquered in the open with many witnesses, making His declaration of a "not guilty" verdict on a sinful mankind valid and indisputable.

Friends, this is excellent news. I am aware that there are many Christians living in fear of demons and devils, but there is no need to fear a defeated foe. Satan has no control over us anymore as the blood of Jesus puts up an eternal partition between him and us. As a matter of fact, if we consider the story of Job, Satan can only touch us with permission from the Father. So, fear not, and stand in the victory that Christ won for us.

Today's Declaration:

I AM SET FREE FROM SATAN'S CONTROL

Day 20

I AM CHOSEN BEFORE THE FOUNDATION OF THE WORLD

For he chose us in him before the creation of the world to be
holy and blameless in his sight. In love he predestined us to
be adopted as his sons through Jesus Christ, in accordance
with his pleasure and will.
Ephesians 1:4

One of the most recent books that I have read, *Journey Back to Heaven,* speaks of the spirits in us that return to God when we die. The author firmly believes that our spirits must have been with God before we were even conceived. Why else would it go back to somewhere it has never been? So, I spent some time searching my memory hoping something would click, and somehow I would remember my existence before conception. Nothing clicked! I will not try to validate this belief though it makes some sense, but you, dear readers, can decide for yourselves.

In any case, it is clear that we were chosen before the foundation of the world. God knew we would be here, right now and in our particular geographical location. Scripture plainly tells us our names were written in the Book of Life before the world was created. It also says our names can be blotted out based on the choices we make during our appointed years. You have a grand opportunity and responsibility to make sure your name remains in that book.

Today's Declaration:

I AM CHOSEN BEFORE THE FOUNDATION OF THE WORLD

Day 21

I AM PREDESTINED TO BE LIKE JESUS

*In him we were also chosen, having been predestined
according to the plan of him who works out everything in
conformity with the purpose of his will.*
Ephesians 1:11

Originally, God's intention for man was a perfect utopia for Him and mankind. Unfortunately, man made a wrong choice that disrupted that plan.

Fortunately, God was still interested in us, even in our fallen state. God still loved us and desired to restore us to our original place in Him. So He became one of us and subjected Himself to the ills and cruelty of our fallen hearts. This effort was twofold. Through Jesus we received grace and salvation, but in Jesus was also the full embodiment of what man was designed to be.

God became the man He intended us to be so we can choose to become the men and women He intended us to be. Jesus was the perfect example and God's original thought when He made the statement, "Let us make man in our own image and likeness" (Genesis 1:26).

Now we can all be like Jesus. Hallelujah!

Today's Declaration:

I AM PREDESTINED TO BE LIKE JESUS

Day 22

I AM FORGIVEN OF ALL MY SINS

When you were dead in your sins and in the
uncircumcision of your sinful nature, God made you alive
with Christ. He forgave us all our sins.
Colossians 2:13

We have a tendency to class sin in different categories. It is interesting that the sin of fornication is considered one of the biggest sins and lying a small sin. Yet in the book of Proverbs, there are seven sins listed that God hates and fornication is not named among them. Lying is! So, if sin has classes, those we see as small are still enormous.

Fortunately, God loves humanity, so He found a way to punish sin and preserve the sinner. Not only that, but in His sovereignty, He punished sins of the past, present, and future. In essence, the sins you have not committed yet have already been paid for. It is done! It is finished!

Christ died for your sins so you can live as God's righteousness. Accept His forgiveness. Believe that you are forgiven and stop wasting precious thoughts on what God has absolutely no memory of. You are forgiven and God remembers your sins no more! To be forgiven is to be declared righteous.

Today's Declaration:

I AM FORGIVEN OF ALL MY SINS

Day 23

I AM WASHED IN THE BLOOD OF THE LAMB

*And from Jesus Christ, who is the faithful witness, the
firstborn from the dead, and the ruler of the kings of the
earth. To him who loves us and has freed us from our sins
by his blood.*
Revelation 1:5

There is power in the blood of Jesus. One profound
revelation of this wonder-working power was in the garden
of gethsemane when He prayed until His sweat became as
blood. If we recall, in the garden of Eden when Adam sinned, one
of the curses pronounced upon him was that "by the sweat of your
brow you will eat your food" (Genesis 3:19). In this garden where
Jesus prayed, His blood redeemed the sweat of our brows,
cancelling even that curse. So yes, because of this, it is possible to
prosper financially without breaking a sweat. Isn't God good?

Now take a look at society and notice what you see. Those
who overwork are usually those who refuse to accept this
wonderful gift of liberty given to us by Christ. So many of us have
taken the high road in this matter, by declaring that we can provide
for ourselves and God is usually not very reliable as it relates to our
needs. Jesus' blood atones for all our sins and curses – we only need
to accept it. The work we need to do is to believe.

The Bible speaks of saints in the latter days whose garments
have been washed in the blood of Jesus. This may seem a terrifying

thought, but it is in fact very liberating – to think that God the Father could look at the sinful man and declare them righteous because of His own blood. To be washed, then, suggests a washing away of all that was deemed unrighteous and impure. In essence, we have been cleansed through and through.

Today's Declaration:

I AM WASHED IN THE BLOOD OF THE LAMB

Day 24

I HAVE A SOUND MIND

*For the Spirit God gave us does not make us timid, but
gives us power, love and self-discipline.*
2 Timothy 1:7

This is especially vital to those of us who suffer from depression, anxiety, and fear. We have to declare this to our minds daily. God is our all-sufficient Father, and we can lean on Him every moment of every day – and some of us have no choice in this matter. In Christ, we have a sound mind.

Paul mentioned in Philippians that we should have the same mind as Christ. Again we see how much "like Christ" we need to be. There is freedom, sanity, and peace in having a sound mind. This is quite liberating in a world of psychiatrists, meditation, yoga, and cognitive behavioral theology that modifies and teaches what the Bible has been saying all these centuries – that our hope can be renewed in Jesus Christ, our true Deliverer. Yes, some measure of freedom and release can be found through the power of our own minds. God did design us to be able to adapt and cope in stressful environments, but He also designed us like Himself. He needs us, and we need Him. It has always been this relational partnership from the very beginning.

I remember Peter walking on the water towards Jesus. Water here signifies life in general: bills, school, work, family, friends, money or the lack thereof. If we keep our eyes on Jesus, we can walk above circumstances and situations. We know what happens if we take our eyes off Jesus.

Our minds need to be renewed daily. Theology and science support the idea that whatever controls the mind control the body. Imagine a mind ruled and saturated by the Word of God. This should be our goal, and I believe these are the ones who Christ spoke to when He said, "They will do even greater things than these" (John 14:12).

Today's Declaration:

I HAVE A SOUND MIND

Day 25

I HAVE THE HOLY SPIRIT

[God] set his seal of ownership on us, and put his Spirit in
our hearts as a deposit, guaranteeing what is to come.
2 Corinthians 1:22

God truly opened my eyes to the fundamental truth in His Word when He said "I will pour out my Spirit upon all flesh."

Jesus was conceived by the Holy Spirit in the womb of a virgin named Mary. He was the second man on Earth to come into existence with a pure soul. Adam was the first. When Adam sinned, his soul died. By extension, we are all born with this dead soul – so there was a need for a second Adam.

Yes, God loved us that much. Through Jesus, He re-created humanity by pouring His Holy Spirit on us the day we became born again. So the same Spirit that was in Christ now lives in us. This also means that whatever Christ did, we can do as well. This brings a whole new meaning to the term, "Christlike."

Sadly, many Christians do not accept this. It sounds good in theory, by practically we still see ourselves as worthless and insignificant creatures trying to squeeze or earn our way into heaven.

The Bible is clear that we are limited only by our faith. If we believe that God will not, then He won't. It is not possible to please and experience God without faith – faith being that confident assurance in who God is and who we are in God.

Knowing and believing in God alone is not enough. Scripture says even demons believe and tremble. To fully walk in the power of the Spirit that Christ has deposited in us requires that we also accept all that He purchased for us at the Cross; accept, above all, that just as Christ is, we are in this world.

Today's Declaration:

I HAVE THE HOLY SPIRIT

Day 26

I AM ADOPTED INTO GOD'S FAMILY

*The Spirit you received does not make you slaves, so that
you live in fear again; rather, the Spirit you received
brought about your adoption to sonship. And by him we
cry, "Abba, Father."*
Romans 8:15

I can't imagine what it is like to be orphaned. I believe it is a
terrible feeling to be abandoned or lose our parents at an early
age with nowhere and no one to turn to.

Even we who are privileged to grow up in a home with both
parents find at times that we feel isolated, abandoned, ignored, and
insignificant. Somehow, throughout the course of our lives, we find
ourselves at a church hearing about a loving Father, who once had
us as a part of His family, but we strayed and were separated from
Him. Now He is calling us back into a relationship with Him.

This is usually hard to accept... a loving yet supreme God,
who is interested in us. It sounds too good to be true, but we
reluctantly follow on to know.

As our knowledge of the Word of God increases, we find
ourselves a part of a new family: God's family. He wants us to call
him "Father," and has made us co-heirs of the kingdom of God
with His Son, Jesus Christ. He says all that He has is ours.

Today's Declaration:

I AM ADOPTED INTO GOD'S FAMILY

Day 27

I AM JUSTIFIED FREELY BY HIS GRACE

*All are justified freely by his grace through the redemption
that came by Christ Jesus.*
Romans 3:24

"Justified" is by far one of my favourite words. To be justified means that I have been declared sinless, just as if I did not sin. This applies to all sins: past, present, and future.

Yes, it can be argued that we are unworthy and undeserving but having the same mind as Christ will open our eyes to the fact that God truly loves us. He could have put conditions on His grace, but He did not. He extended His love to us free of cost. Sin separates us from God, and if God dealt with our sin by becoming sin and crucifying it to the cross, then He wanted to remove that element that separated us from Him. We no longer have to live isolated from God. We no longer have to exist outside of a relationship with our Creator.

But we can still be separated from Him if we reject His work in our minds, if we think we don't deserve to be justified by grace and continue to walk in condemnation. That is not what God wants for us. God bids us come, sit, and dine with Him. He has paid the price to make this all possible. We simply need to believe.

Today's Declaration:

I AM JUSTIFIED FREELY BY HIS GRACE

Day 28

I HAVE ALL THINGS PERTAINING TO LIFE

His divine power has given us everything we need for a
godly life through our knowledge of him who called us by
his own glory and goodness.
2 Peter 1:3

I think it is clear that outside of Christ we can do nothing. Jesus said so in His discourse on the side of the mountain. On the other hand, with Him all things are possible.

Jesus was fully man, yet fully divine. He did a work that not many Christians have applied to their lives or accepted. He did a complete work in restoring us to our former glory. If we can understand that, then we know that all that belongs to Him also belongs to us.

We were dead before God came to Earth and died in our place. Our only life is in Christ. There is no life outside of Christ regardless of what we think or feel. If we were dead, and God gave us His life, then the life we now possess really don't belong to us. His divine power has given us everything we need to live and live in a godly way. Therefore, the only two options we have are life and death. If our desire is to live, then our choice must be Jesus Christ because He is life.

Today's Declaration:

I HAVE ALL THINGS PERTAINING TO LIFE

Day 29

I HAVE GREAT AND PRECIOUS PROMISES

*Through these he has given us his very great and precious
promises, so that through them you may participate in the
divine nature, having escaped the corruption in the world
caused by evil desires.*
2 Peter 1:4

I love to read and declare God's promises, though at times it
can get a little frustrating when God doesn't move on my
schedule. In reality, it is only His timing that matters. It is
always perfect, as God sees the whole picture while we see only
parts. His promises are sure, and in this book you will find many of
them that you can cling to.

There is a saying that faith will speak things that are not as if
they are. This is a fundamental principle we must adopt as we learn
God's promises, some of which are applicable with conditions.
That is, there is something we need to do before we can claim
God's promises.

I will share a revelation with you as it relates to tithing and
giving. God promises that if we give and tithe, He will open the
windows of heaven and pour such a blessing out that we will not
have room to receive it. This promise is one I claim for my life, but
I have not been faithful on my part. I sow tithes inconsistently,
often borrowing it for more immediate needs, yet I could not

understand what happened to the outpouring God had promised on occasions that I did pay my tithe.

The Father spoke to me one day. He said my inconsistency has caused my lands to be dry and desolate, so on the occasions where I was obedient, and He poured out blessings... the dry ground would soak up the water quickly. He made it clear that it would take a little while for the ground to be saturated and for me to experience that overflow.

This is a familiar example of a spiritual principle. He instructed me to double my tithes and to keep sowing it until I eventually experience the overflow.

His promises are sure, but we lack or fail to experience the fullness of what God has for us because of our disobedience. The good news is that if we do what God says, we have full rights to claim His promises, which are great and precious. He promises health, wealth, and prosperity to those who are obedient to Him. If we abide in Christ, and His Word abides in us, then anything we ask for we will receive. Anything! This is a fact. Only wayward sons and daughters will not experience the fullness of God's promises, and He desires to bless us. He takes pleasure in pouring out on us, but we often rob Him of that pleasure because we fail to do what He says. Through His promises, we partake of His divine nature. We will experience God's supernatural manifestations in our lives. The Word says that the pure in heart will see God.

Today's Declaration:

I HAVE GREAT AND PRECIOUS PROMISES

Day 30

I HAVE A MINISTRY OF RECONCILIATION

All this is from God, who reconciled us to himself through
Christ and gave us the ministry of reconciliation.
2 Corinthians 5:18

Through sin, we were made enemies of God. All of us were born as God's enemies. Therefore, there is a need for reconciliation. Reconciliation is not something we accomplish on our merit and strength, but it is only possible through Jesus. As we look at the world today, we see many who are living out their lives not giving much thought to being reconciled with God. They may not even see an urgent need to do so. This is sad because one day each of us will stand before God, whether we believe it or not. Our thoughts and beliefs do not matter in light of the truth. If we think there is no judgment, the fact that there will be a judgment remains unchanged.

Here is where it gets fascinating. As you examine the state of mankind throughout history, a majority of us have cared very little to be reconciled with God. We could not fit an invisible God into our intellect, so we choose to disregard the very thought of His existence. It was in this state that God made the bold move of sending His Son into this world to take our place. We did not ask Him to.

If it were up to us entirely, we would just live our lives and then go to hell, not sure how we got there. But God has been reaching down to mankind from the very first time Adam sinned. He never stopped. He gave us the laws, the Ark of the Covenant, prophets, kings, and finally, Himself.

Take heart. Like me, you sometimes feel like God is not there or may not be hearing you when you pray. He may seem distant, and you may even feel abandoned by the Almighty, but this is never the case.

For 400 years, the Israelites were slaves in Egypt. They were taunted and ridiculed, but God showed up. For 400 years, there was silence from God between the end of the Old Testament and the beginning of the New, but God showed up. Several months or years of not hearing from God is a small price to pay, but God will show up. History says that He always does, and He always will. He has reconciled us to Himself through Jesus Christ. We are no longer enemies of God, but friends.

Today's Declaration:

I HAVE A MINISTRY OF RECONCILIATION

Day 31

I HAVE AUTHORITY OVER THE POWER OF THE ENEMY

*I have given you authority to trample on snakes and
scorpions and to overcome all the power of the enemy;
nothing will harm you.*
Luke 10:19

I know this is difficult to believe. The enemy seems so strong, and we feel powerless against his attacks, but again we are limited only by what we believe. If we see ourselves as weaker than the enemy, even in Christ, then we will appear to be weaker. This is because if we doubt what God says about us, we essentially call Him a liar. It is important that we accept and receive everything God reveals about us in His Word. Calling Him a liar will render us powerless.

Christ died on the cross. Death had a temporary victory, but when He took up His lifeless body after three days and declared it alive again, He conquered death, hell, and the grave. In conquering this three-headed giant, He formed a key and put that key in our hands, giving us full authority over death, hell, and the grave. The problem is, we have the key, but we don't know how to use it.

Jesus said that a small measure of faith can move a physical mountain. Be honest: do you think you can speak to a mountain, and have it move out of its place and cast itself into the sea? Many have interpreted this verse symbolically. "Jesus was not referring to a physical mountain," we may say. But he spoke this right after he had spoken to a natural fig tree, and it died from the roots. The mountain will move, if you believe it will.

Likewise, the enemy has no power over us. He did once, even when we were under the law...but under grace that power is broken. The Bible says Jesus made a public spectacle of them, meaning there were witnesses who made this event an indisputable fact. When the enemy comes against us like a flood, our Father will lift up a standard against him.

Do not be fooled by the Devils subtlety and crafty words. His greatest deception in Christendom is convincing born again believers that he still has power over them. He is lying. There is no truth in him. Declare it until you believe in your spirit and mind that...

Today's Declaration:

I HAVE AUTHORITY OVER THE POWER OF THE ENEMY

Day 32

I HAVE ACCESS TO THE SECRET PLACE OF GOD

*In him and through faith in him we may approach God
with freedom and confidence.*
Ephesians 3:12

There is no higher privilege than the access we have been given into the holy of holies where the presence of God resides. In the past, only a perfect and sinless priest could go into the holy of holies. Those on the outside had to tie a rope around his waist or ankle to pull him out, just in case he entered with sin.

No man had access to God directly, but Jesus changed that. When He died, the veil in the temple was torn in two, signifying full access to the throne of God. We are covered in Christ's blood and declared children of God, so we can come boldly to the throne of grace. Christ has elevated us from servants to sons and daughters of the most high God, and given us direct access to our Abba (Father)!

David partook of this long before it became a reality in time. He writes: "He who dwells in the secret place of the Most High Shall abide under the shadow of the Almighty." (Psalm 91:1 – NKJV).

Every believer have access to the secret place of God.

Today's Declaration:

I HAVE ACCESS TO THE SECRET PLACE OF GOD

Day 33

I HAVE WISDOM

*In him we have redemption through his blood, the
forgiveness of sins, in accordance with the riches of God's
grace that he lavished on us with all wisdom and
understanding.
Ephesians 1:7-8*

*I keep asking that the God of our Lord Jesus Christ, the
glorious Father, may give you the Spirit of wisdom and
revelation, so that you may know him better.
Ephesians 1:17*

Solomon was given a grand opportunity to ask Father God
for anything he wanted. He did not seem to have spent a
great deal of time thinking about it but knew exactly what he
wanted. He asked for wisdom. Because of this request, we have
been given a book called Proverbs that is filled with wisdom
regarding our relationships with God and each other.

James was a brother to Jesus. He knew the Son of God from
childhood, and at one point he did not believe that Jesus was the
Messiah. Eventually, all was revealed, and James wrote about
wisdom. He thought it was important enough for all Christians to
possess and declared that those who lack it should ask God for it,
and if we do, not to doubt that we will receive it.

There are many schools of thought on this topic, but one that stands out is this: Knowledge, wisdom, and understanding usually travel together. Knowledge can be acquired through study, experience, and divine revelation. Wisdom and understanding are what we do with that acquired knowledge.

In Christ, we lack no good thing. If we lack wisdom, it is because we haven't asked for it.

Today's Declaration:

I HAVE WISDOM

Day 34

I AM COMPLETE IN HIM

*And in Christ you have been brought to fullness. He is the
head over every power and authority.*
Colossians 2:10

To say that we are complete in Christ is to also say that outside of Christ we were incomplete. This is a sobering thought. I have seen countless testimonies of drug addicts, prostitutes, and criminals who have come to the saving knowledge and power of Jesus Christ. They all have the same testimony. No matter how much is achieved and how much money is earned, there is a void that cannot be filled by anything or anyone but God. This makes sense: we all came out of God, so only He can complete us.

Atheists are those who have accepted incompleteness and found a way to live with it, but even they know there is something out there that they have chosen to ignore. The very definition of "atheist" suggests an awareness of God. It is just that they choose not to believe in Him.

We who believe in Christ also accept that in Him we have found completeness. In essence, He completes us.

Today's Declaration:

I AM COMPLETE IN HIM

Day 35

I AM FREE FOREVER FROM SIN'S POWER

*For sin shall no longer be your master, because you are not
under law, but under grace.*
Romans 6:14

Paul spoke in depth about the law and its purposes. He had the authority and experience to do so. He had walked under the law and grace, so he was familiar with both sides. Before his experience on the road to Damascus, he persecuted Christians, believing he was acting on the will of God. The Father met him and converted him. Paul's writings are still foundational for the church today.

Paul said that the law had a purpose: it revealed sin but could not atone for it. In other words, if it were not for the law, we would not know what sin is.

The definition of sin is disobedience to God. There is no sin that is not a violation of God's way and instructions to mankind. Adam was told not to eat of a particular tree. The sin was not eating but doing something God said not to do. Adam's sin was disobedience, and we are all paying the price for that act of rebellion.

The law became necessary then. Obedience to it was a sign of a heart willing to follow God. The law also revealed the necessity of a Redeemer. If not for the law, we would not see a reason for a

Messiah. That is why the scriptures say Jesus came to fulfil the law. In Him, the law was complete, and the power of sin broken forever.

Even though we fall from time to time, it doesn't mean that sin has somehow regained its power over us. Sadly, we have to live with our fallen nature until Jesus completes the work He started, but know that you sin, not from the perspective of who you are now in Christ, but from the point of view of your old self that is dead in Christ.

Today's Declaration:

I AM FREE FOREVER FROM SIN'S POWER

Day 36

I AM SANCTIFIED

And that is what some of you were. But you were washed,
you were sanctified, you were justified in the name of the
Lord Jesus Christ and by the Spirit of our God.
1 Corinthians 6:11

When we examined this concept in length in Bible study, it led to some interesting arguments. The definition of "sanctified" is to be set apart as holy or to be cleansed. This denotes a cleansing of our old nature from the inside out. There are varying beliefs on whether sanctification is a onetime process or a lifelong experience. Some subscribe to both, others one or the other. What matters is how sanctification is achieved. Jesus said He sanctifies us through His Word. We are cleansed by the Word of God.

Let us accept that if the Bible is just a book that we read, there will be absolutely no benefit from that. The Word needs to leave the page and enter our minds and spirits. How this is achieved is through faith.

One of the issues we have today is that we read the Word, but we do not believe it. We see Jesus raising the dead, and we say, "Well, that is not possible in this day and age, even though Jesus also said 'greater things shall we do.'" We should understand why it is not possible to please God without faith.

Sanctification is a work of the Holy Spirit that begins at the moment of our spiritual rebirth. Whether it is a one-time work or a lifelong process is beside the point. It needs to be maintained throughout our Christian walk, which suggests that we can lose our sanctification.

Some have testified that they felt different, others have felt nothing, but in a natural sense, sanctification can be likened to a detoxification of the body. It is God's work to purge and wash us, and declare us clean.

Today's Declaration:

I AM SANCTIFIED

Day 37

I AM FIT FOR THE MASTER'S USE

In a large house there are articles not only of gold and silver, but also of wood and clay; some are for special purposes and some for common use. Those who cleanse themselves from the latter will be instruments for special purposes, made holy, useful to the Master and prepared to do any good work.
2 Timothy 2:20-21

We have a level of responsibility to each other that is mostly ignored. We are our brothers' keepers. The fact that we fell through sin, thereby losing all interest in God, suggests that we are in trouble.

I was standing in a cemetery recently, and God ministered to me there. I realized that there were many dreams, businesses, and unmet goals buried there, but I also realized that that could not be the end. We are eternal beings. Though some of us will die and ultimately end up in a coffin underground, there is that part of us that lives on in the real realm.

It is amazing that the actual reality is the world we cannot see with our natural eyes. Here is a reality check for us: people need to be born again. They need to be saved. If they are not saved before they die, they will have to spend eternity in a very unpleasant place. This is where we make ourselves available so God can save as many humans as He possibly can through us.

It is sad that many of us are contented with just being saved. We accept that each person has a personal responsibility to his or her soul and their choice has nothing to do with us. On the contrary – their choice has everything to do with us! We are the instruments God uses to bring salvation to the lost. How can we be contented with being saved when our family, friends, and co-workers are not? Can we just sit by and shrug our shoulders while those we love go to hell? Most Christians do not intentionally witness. All Christians should witness.

Understanding who we are in Christ should guide, even determine, our actions. We cannot know the Master wants to use us to save others and consciously deny Him that privilege.

Today's Declaration:

I AM FIT FOR THE MASTER'S USE

Day 38

I AM LOVED ETERNALLY

*This inheritance is kept in heaven for you, who through
faith are shielded by God's power until the coming of the
salvation that is ready to be revealed in the last time.*
1 Peter 1:4-5

If God can step from His kairos (God's eternal time) into our Chronos (man's time), then He must love us. If He would come to Earth as a man to stop the hand of the devil from striking his final blow, then He must truly love us. If He could allow Himself to be stripped naked, beaten, ridiculed, spit on, punched, kicked and abused, then He must love us. Can we deny such a love?

To be loved eternally is to be loved completely. There is no greater love… and this love was extended to us while we were still unborn and not yet conceived sinners.

We sometimes walk in condemnation because of sin. God had loved you before you sinned, and He loves you with equal intensity, if not more, now. As a matter of fact, He said the more you sin, is the more grace you will receive.

Does this mean we should sin more? No! It means that we are covered. All the sin that you will commit in your entire life has been paid for in full, so death is no longer a consequence we have to be subjected to. "Father forgive me," is enough to remain in our Father's love.

When Adam sinned, God knew. Still, He came to him, asking, "Adam, where are you?" God was looking for him, even knowing that he has just pronounced a death sentence on the whole human race. That's love!

God loves you and has loved you since before the world was created, when you were just a thought in His mind. He lovingly wrote each of our names in the book of life, before the foundations of the earth. It is up to us to abide in that love.

Today's Declaration:

I AM LOVED ETERNALLY

Day 39

I AM ETERNALLY KEPT IN THE PALM OF HIS HAND

My Father, who has given them to me, is greater than all;
no one can snatch them out of my Father's hand.
John 10:29

J esus once made the profound statement that not one of those the Father had given Him was lost, except the son of perdition.

There are many Christians around the world struggling with sin. A lot of them are wondering if, like that son of perdition, they were born to go to hell or born to fail. Our Father loves each of us equally and knows how to take care of His own. None of us will be lost at the end of this age. Jesus will make sure of that.

Acts 17:28 - "For in him we live and move and have our being." As some of your own poets have said, "We are his offspring."

We belong to God, and nothing can change that. We are called by His name and sealed by His blood and promise. In the palm of God's hand, we have found rest for all time.

"Eternity" is a word or concept that is easily misunderstood. We see this as a future period of existence, but we are wrong. Eternity has always existed, before time itself. Time as we know it is a small part of eternity. The beginning for us is not the beginning for God, who has no beginning. We have a beginning, and He is our end. For us, the Father is truly the Alpha and the Omega.

Eternity was in existence long before Genesis 1 and it will continue long after Revelation 22. Our existence is just one chapter in God's book, and we are privileged now that we exist, to continue existing for all time.

Being in Christ is being in the palm of God's hand forever.

Though we had a beginning, we will never see an end.

Today's Declaration:

I AM ETERNALLY KEPT IN THE PALM OF HIS HAND

Day 40

I AM KEPT FROM FALLING

To him who is able to keep you from falling and to present you before his glorious presence without fault and with great joy.
Jude 1:24

Is it possible to live as a born-again believer and not sin? This question has been asked numerous times in Bible study, and the answers differ. We are drawn to a passage that tells us we should "walk in the spirit, and we will not satisfy the lust of the flesh" (Galatians 5:16). This suggests that it may not be possible to sin while walking in the Spirit. I would think most people would agree with this.

Walking in the Spirit denotes obedience to God. The definition of sin is disobedience to God. There is no sin that is not a direct rebellion against God's laws. I am not talking about the law that could not save, but the commands that we are to live by, demonstrating our love for God. He said if we love Him, we will keep His commandments.

The conclusion is, it is not possible to walk in obedience and disobedience to God simultaneously. When we walk in His Spirit, we are indeed kept from falling.

Today's Declaration:

I AM KEPT FROM FALLING

Day 41

I AM KEPT BY THE POWER OF GOD

Who through faith are shielded by God's power until the coming of the salvation that is ready to be revealed in the last time.
1 Peter 1:5

I think one of the most crucial lessons that most Christians learn on this journey is just how hard it is. Jesus said if we are to follow Him, we must deny ourselves and take up our crosses.

This sounds good in theory but is hard in practice. Denying oneself or dying to oneself is painful and debilitating, yet very necessary. Only when we stop fighting our battles and trying to make our own way do we see the full manifestation of God's power in our lives. As long as we try to do it on our own, we will only see our power, which is not much on the grander scale.

So life gets complicated. We incur debts, people we know and love die, we get sick, and sometimes our infirmities appear incurable or doctors are unable to diagnose them. We lose our jobs or just do not make enough money to cover expenses. We get in car accidents, fight the urge to use pornography and drugs, and get into fights with severe consequences. Yes, life can get tough. Christians go to prison for manslaughter because of reckless driving that takes a life.

It is hard for us to see God's hand in our lives during these most trying times but understand that on our own strength and power we would be unable to make it through any of this. It is by God's power that we have survived and continue to live through the rough times. Where is God in all these situations? He is walking you through it. The downside is that we may be unable to see it until we come out on the other side and look back.

Rest assured that no matter what you are going through right now, the power of God is being demonstrated in your life and God will not leave you for a second in your pain and distress. He will take you through it. He will give you just as much as you can bear, and He will carry the rest.

Today's Declaration:

I AM KEPT BY THE POWER OF GOD

Day 42

I AM NOT CONDEMNED

Therefore, there is now no condemnation for those who are in Christ Jesus, because through Christ Jesus the law of the Spirit who gives life has set you free from the law of sin and death.
Romans 8:1-2

This was very liberating for me. There was a time in my Christian walk when I was fornicating, masturbating, and watching porn weekly… maybe daily… maybe more than once a day. It was a difficult time for me as I did not have the heart to walk away from God's presence for sin. I resorted to begging forgiveness every time I prayed, but the guilt and sense of condemnation were overwhelming. Though I was in God, I could not face Him out of shame and embarrassment as an addict to sin. I was naked and ashamed.

In essence, I was having this difficult time coming face to face with the very One—the only One—who could set me free, and He did.

Now that I look back, I understand a little better and can minister to those who have found themselves where I was. God never condemns us and try to make us feel guilty. He is a loving God; caring, warm, and welcoming. Those sins that have you bound, He nailed them all to the cross before you committed them…long before the act of your conception.

When Adam sinned, God came looking for him. It is the same with us today. Condemnation and guilt are weapons of the devil, but no weapon formed against us can prosper. Christ died for sinners, not saints, so go to Him. He is looking for you, calling out to you. Rebuke those spirits of condemnation and guilt and run to your loving Father. He is waiting to embrace you, forgive you, and set you free. Let principalities and powers know that...

Today's Declaration:

I AM NOT CONDEMNED

Day 43

I AM ONE WITH THE LORD

But whoever is united with the Lord is one with him in
spirit.
1 Corinthians 6:17

The same Spirit who raised Christ from the dead lives in you and me. Allow me to give you an even deeper revelation. Jesus Christ is the Word become flesh (See John 1:1-2). This means, He is the Word spoken in Genesis that created all things. God spoke, and it was.

Jesus, the Father, and the Holy Spirit are one. Jesus dwells in us through His Holy Spirit. God lives in us through the Holy Spirit. So the very Word that created all things at the very beginning lives inside you and me.

I pray that as you read this book, you do it out loud and begin to declare these truths over your lives. This is a fact! That is why we have the power of life and death in our very tongues. It matters what you say. We struggle because we have been believing and saying the wrong things.

Jesus lives in us through His Spirit. This makes us one with Him in spirit. We are like God. Through Him, we can do all things. Outside of Him, we can do nothing. This means what we do is what God does. If we can only do it with God, it means it is God doing it. When we become one with Him, He lives through us and enables us to walk in the supernatural.

We err when we begin to accept the glory for the things we can do, and the wisdom that falls from our lips on occasion, because there is no glory in it for us. We are one with God in spirit. Paul says it perfectly, "I no longer live, but Christ lives in me" (Galatians 2:20).

Today's Declaration:

I AM ONE WITH THE LORD

Day 44

I AM BORN FROM HEAVEN

*Jesus answered, "I am the way and the truth and the life.
No one comes to the Father except through me."*
John 14:6

As a young man growing up, I never liked going to funerals. I thought it was a noble gesture to refuse to plant a corpse in my mind as the last image of someone I knew. People die, I told myself. Some go to heaven. Others – perhaps most – go to hell. It is life.

Now I am wiser, having experienced the death of my father. When it hits home, reality can blow your mind. I found absolutely no comfort in the fact that my father was saved and on his way to heaven. It is hard to be comforted when you stand over an open casket and see a lifeless body unable to communicate or respond to you in any way. But it is sobering to know that the real person who animated the physical body is absent, but still in existence.

The reality of heaven is not always comforting, but it is the truth. I am not sure how to reconcile such glory with the reality of death. It was a sad three days for the disciples back in Jerusalem after Jesus died. They knew He was the Son of God, but they also knew that he was physically dead. Seemingly, there was no life in death. But the same body that was wounded and marred beyond recognition was renewed and rose from the dead in our time and space. The same can be said of Lazarus and many dead saints who burst out of their tombs when Jesus died.

Elijah's bone touched the corpse of a man long dead, and that man sprang to life. So here is a new reality for us to digest. We are not just on our way to heaven, but we are already there because we were born from there. One mystic says it like this, "You cannot return to somewhere you have never been originally." In Christ, though we may die, we live. We are citizens of heaven, and if we can fully grasp this revelation, we will see that even death has no power over us. It is simply a step into our true and glorified existence.

Today's Declaration:

I AM BORN FROM HEAVEN

Day 45

I AM QUICKENED BY HIS MIGHTY POWER

*But if the Spirit of him that raised up Jesus from the dead
dwell in you, he that raised up Christ from the dead shall
also quicken your mortal bodies by his Spirit that dwelleth
in you. (Romans 8:11).*

Ephesians 2:1 says, "And you hath he quickened, who were
dead in trespasses and sins." "Quicken" is an interesting
word that in this context means, "to make alive," but of
course in modern speech also means "to make faster." Would it
surprise us if God wanted to accelerate our cleansing and
purification from sin? We can only be made clean through His
power.

In this world, there are many "powers." People can do
extraordinary things as part of the real, spiritual world. When
Moses first went to Pharaoh, he threw down his staff, and it
became a snake; Pharaoh had people who could do the same thing,
yet not through God. So, when Scripture refers to our God, we will
hear terms like "God of gods," "Lord of lords," "King of kings,"
"Everlasting Father," and "Mighty Power." The choice of
adjectives suggests superiority and authenticity.

To say we are quickened by His mighty power is to admit that
His power can do for us what no other power can.

Today's Declaration:

I AM QUICKENED BY HIS MIGHTY POWER

Day 46

I AM SEATED WITH CHRIST IN HEAVENLY PLACES

Blessed be the God and Father of our Lord Jesus Christ, who hath blessed us with all spiritual blessings in heavenly places in Christ.
Ephesians 1:3

And God raised us up with Christ and seated us with him in the heavenly realms in Christ Jesus. (Ephesians 2:6).

Sometimes we base our ideas of who we are on gravity. Our feet are firmly planted on the Earth, and we fail to see that as born-again believers we exist in two realms: the natural and the supernatural. Most people are contented going through their entire lives in the natural, but there are those of us who desire the supernatural.

The Word of God says that "God raised us up with Christ and seated us with him in the heavenly realms" (Ephesians 2:6). This is worthy of declaration but let us not miss the real meaning.

We often sing in church that satan is under our feet while stomping our feet on the ground. If this were the reality of it, then the devil would surely be as flat as a pancake by now. Yes, he is under our feet, but not in that sense.

Jesus put principalities and powers to shame. He took the key of death, hell, and the grave and handed the keys of the Kingdom to us. His sacrifice exalted Him high above all principalities and powers and gave Him a name above all other names. He is elevated above all, which makes everything practically below His feet. If we are indeed seated with Him in the heavenly realms as co-heirs or joint heirs, then everything under Jesus' feet is also under ours. We are royalty in this Earth. We are kings in this Earth. As Christ is, so are we. Declare it! Believe it!

Today's Declaration:

I AM SEATED WITH CHRIST IN HEAVENLY PLACES

Day 47

I AM THE HEAD AND NOT THE TAIL

*The Lord will make you the head, not the tail. If you pay
attention to the commands of the Lord your God that I
give you this day and carefully follow them, you will always
be at the top, never at the bottom.*
Deuteronomy 28:13

I was sitting in a theology class when this came up. Some argued that this is not relevant to us today as God was speaking to the Israelites. We all know they are God's chosen; His first-born. The argument continued that Jesus is the head, and the church is His body, so there is no other head but Him. If the church were full of heads, it would be a multi-head monster with no body.

I agree to some extent that Jesus is the head, and there is no other. The context in which we view this position is more symbolic than figurative, though it can be argued further. To say we are the head is to say God has placed us in a higher position than the tail, and we all know the position of a tail.

As children of god, we are elevated above principalities and powers, rulers of the darkness of this age, spiritual wickedness in high places, and essentially time, space, and matter. This position allows us to walk in the supernatural. It puts us in a position of authority, confidence, and assurance that God is the highest power, and He lives in us, making all that seemed impossible possible.

In reality, we should be the head of corporations, the head of parliament, the head of social justice, and so on. That is our rightful place though most Christians settle for far less. If we do not occupy our proper places, then the enemy has the right to set his people there. The result of that is that we end up working for non-Christians and being accountable to those who have no fear of God. It really should be the other way around.

Today's Declaration:

I AM THE HEAD AND NOT THE TAIL

Day 48

I AM LIGHT IN THE DARKNESS

*You are the light of the world. A town built on a hill
cannot be hidden.*
Matthew 5:14

I love this concept. The very first Word that our Father spoke was, "Let there be light." We read further that Jesus is the light of the world. The "light" has always been in existence.

It is believed that we were once covered in a glorious celestial light before we fell into sin. This resulted in us walking in darkness, but God had the ultimate plan of redemption for us all. He had every intention of restoring our light. This was made possible through the death and resurrection of Jesus Christ. In Christ, we are also the light of the world.

Let us deepen our understanding of the purpose of light. We have day because of light. If there were an absence of light, there would be nothing but darkness. We think of day and night as separate, but the day only exists because light exist.

Imagine this world without light. Imagine this world without Christians. Non-Christians will deny that this world still turns because of us. We often fail to see this critical fact ourselves. There is coming a day when this world will once again see darkness.

In Matthew, we read where the sun will be darkened, the moon will turn blood red, and the stars will fall from their place. The world will be plunged into utter darkness. Why? An absence of light will result in darkness. While we are here, let us shine our lights as brightly as possible. The world needs us, so let us light it up.

Today's Declaration:

I AM LIGHT IN THE DARKNESS

Day 49

I AM A CANDLE IN A DARK PLACE

*Neither do people light a lamp and put it under a bowl.
Instead they put it on its stand, and it gives light to
everyone in the house.*
Matthew 5:15

Some translations use "candle" instead of "lamp." A candle illuminates a much smaller area than a lamp. It is more accurate and centered. I think this is suggestive of the role we should play in our homes, and in the lives of our families.

Sometimes we are the reason our family members do not get saved because our lives at home and our lives at church differ. The tone we use when we talk to our church family is different from the tone we use when we talk to our natural family, especially those not yet saved. This seldom goes unnoticed, and we need to be more mindful of this. Our responsibility in their lives is to provide enough light that they can see the truth. If we fail to do this, we run the risk of losing them for all eternity.

Many Christians do a better job at saving strangers than their families. Very often, our tolerance is lowest when it comes to those closest to us. We react to their stubbornness with ridicule and impatience. We cannot put a greater effort in saving strangers than those who are related to us. We are the candle in their darkness. What profit is there if that candle is lit and hidden under a bowl?

As our path was once illuminated, let us seek to light the way for those closest to us. It may take more effort, but what other hope is there for them if our candles are not burning bright and consistent enough to show them the way?

Today's Declaration:

I AM A CANDLE IN A DARK PLACE

Day 50

I AM A CITY SET ON A HILL

*You are the light of the world. A town built on a hill
cannot be hidden.*
Matthew 5:14

Some representatives of Christ are afraid to be identified with Christ. In the workplace, we may try to keep a low profile. In schools, we try to fit in with the crowd with a watered-down version of our commitment to Christ.

I remember that in high school, very few who were saved lived out that salvation at school. There was one particular girl who cursed, lied, and was known to fornicate openly – this is in direct contradiction to who she was at home. But can we hide who we are? Why would we be ashamed to be identified as a Christian?

We need to know who we are. Christianity seemed like something personal that should be kept hidden to avoid unnecessary attention and questions. But Jesus welcomed all that. It is usually through those means that He was able to minister to so many.

We should be different in our speech and action from the rest of the world. People should notice and ask us about it. The apostles told us always to be ready to give an answer to everyone for the hope that we have (See 1 Peter 3:15). If we are a city on a hill, there is no use trying to hide. Our attempts at not being seen will be in direct contradiction to who we are, and our witness will be destroyed. The world can tell the difference between those who belong to Christ and those who pretend.

Be the city on a hill that will draw all who see you to Jesus Christ. What greater purpose do we serve in the Kingdom?

Today's Declaration:

I AM A CITY SET ON A HILL

Day 51

I AM THE SALT OF THE EARTH

You are the salt of the earth. But if the salt loses its
saltiness, how can it be made salty again? It is no longer
good for anything, except to be thrown out and trampled
underfoot.
Matthew 5:13

This is how important we are in this world. The world chooses to be ignorant of the fact that if this Earth had no Christians, then there would only be chaos and destruction. Think of the time when Jesus made His appearance on Earth. Rome was at war with the Jews, and every other nation was at war. In the temple, sacrifices were still being made according to the law, but there was no righteousness or justice (See Amos).

Jesus actually did change the world. The sad part for me is that He did not find His disciples in the Church. If we are not careful, history will repeat itself, and a time will return when the Earth has no salt.

We can tolerate this world because we provide the salt that gives life its taste. We set the trends, provide the foundation for morals and values, and create a balance between the evil we desire and the righteousness that Jesus Christ provides. Wherever we are, there should be a noticeable difference. We do not respond to challenges the way the world does, and our speech is supported by all the wisdom and knowledge that heaven affords us. More and more companies are seeing the need to hire Christians because of their integrity, commitment, and dedication. Yes, there are those who give us a bad name, but no one is perfect in and of themselves. There is hope, even for those who are unstable and double-minded.

The world survives because of you. Keep adding that unique flavor in your workplaces, schools, and communities.

Today's Declaration:

I AM THE SALT OF THE EARTH

Day 52

I AM HIS SHEEP

*I am the good shepherd; I know my sheep and my sheep
know me.*
John 10:14

Jesus Christ is our Shepherd and refers to us accordingly. This
suggests that we are well taken care of. The relationship that
exists between the shepherd and sheep is one to be admired.

A young man was watching two different sets of sheep go into
one pen. All the sheep looked alike, and he wondered how the
shepherd would know which sheep belonged to him the following
day. The young man made sure to be there the next day. The first
shepherd came to the pen and made a distinctive sound. All his
sheep came out and followed him. This was an amazing
demonstration of what Jesus referred to in John 10:14. His sheep
know His voice.

Many Christians struggle today with distinguishing God's
voice from all the other voices in their heads. I propose that there
are always several voices present: the voice of the self, the voice of
the shepherd, the voice of the father of lies, etc. If we understand
these distinct voices, we will learn to hear God when He speaks.

The father of lies is just that: a liar. He may tell half-truths like
he did in the garden of Eden, but he speaks mostly lies. He is the
reason you believe that you are nobody, worthless, insignificant,
and unworthy to be called a son of God, but it is all lies.

The Spirit of Truth knows your every thought, and the Shepherd can respond to what you are thinking. It is possible to know the voice of the Shepherd. The responsibility that remains now is for us to consciously obey His voice. When God called Moses and gave him instructions, Moses told God to find somebody else. This angered the Lord. If you want to know your Shepherd, be prepared to obey Him.

Today's Declaration:

I AM HIS SHEEP

Day 53

I AM A CITIZEN OF HEAVEN

*For our citizenship is in heaven, from which we also eagerly
wait for the Savior, the Lord Jesus Christ. (Philippians
3:20 - NKJV).*

A citizen of heaven… I grew up believing that this was a future state of existence. I would live my life trying to make good choices and hopefully, when I died and stood before God, He would see enough to permit me into heaven. This theology is wrong.

Heaven is now. Jesus mentioned that the Kingdom of heaven was at hand before He died. When He rose from the dead, the Kingdom of heaven was fully established here on Earth. What this means is that the partition that sin created between heaven and Earth was utterly destroyed. If we are not citizens of heaven now, we will not be citizens of heaven if or when we die.

The Word says we are seated with Christ in the heavenly realms. As Jesus is now, so are we right now. Who we are in Christ is not bound by time, space, or matter. It is an eternal reality for each of us. We are in heaven right now with Christ.

Yes, we exist in two realms: the natural and the supernatural. Most Christians will live out their entire lives only in the physical. They will not experience the healing, miracles, and prosperity that are afforded to us in the realm of the spiritual. In the natural we may be sick, but in the supernatural we are well. It is for us to declare it, thank God for it, and speak it until that becomes our reality. Some will; some may not. We can live in the natural and still be saved, but we miss the fullness of what Christ has done for us and how we are to function in the world.

Jesus said it best, "We are in the world, but not of the world." In essence, our citizenship is elsewhere. We should not fear death. It has no power over us. We will be transfigured. Death is a divine design that can only usher us into our rightful home. Death is the end of all trouble, grief, temptations, pain, sickness, and tears. It is the beginning of a new life in a world where sin does not exist.

Today's Declaration:

I AM A CITIZEN OF HEAVEN

Day 54

I AM HIDDEN WITH CHRIST IN GOD

You are my hiding place; you will protect me from trouble
and surround me with songs of deliverance.
Psalm 32:7

I doubt any of us has seen the level of trouble David experienced during his lifetime, yet he could declare that a man will see many troubles, but God delivers him from them all. How was he able to make that declaration? Only because he saw many difficulties, and he was delivered from them all.

We may not have periods in our lives where someone set above us will try to kill us, or our son tries to overthrow us, or we murder one of our friends because we got their wife pregnant, or countless life-threatening battles with giants and bloodthirsty enemies that want nothing more than to trample on our corpses. In contrast to David's life, we have little to deal with and much to give thanks for. His words resonate with us today, despite our circumstances. They are read during devotions at church, and during praise and worship. His words comfort us in our darkest hours. David still did not have what we have today. Yes, he dwelt in the secret place of the most high God, but now the most high God dwells in us.

Today's Declaration:

I AM HIDDEN WITH CHRIST IN GOD

Day 55

I AM PROTECTED FROM THE EVIL ONE

We know that anyone born of God does not continue to
sin; the one who was born of God keeps them safe, and the
evil one cannot harm him.
1 John 5:18

Job was a man living the "American dream." He had sons and daughters, flocks, servants, a good wife and a fortune. He was a God-fearing man who walked in health and prosperity, but his uprightness did not go unnoticed.

Satan went to God for permission to test Job. This turned Job's life into a heart-wrenching experience that none of us would want to share.

Luckily, we got to see all sides of the story. In our lives, we will not see satan asking permission or the boundaries that God has set. All we would see is our children dying, our flocks dying, our wife or husband leaving, and the sickness in our body that seems to come out of nowhere. Could we say, like Job, "The Lord gave and the Lord has taken away; may the name of the Lord be praised?" (Job 1:21).

But let us not miss the most important part of the story. Satan needed permission to touch Job, just as he needs permission to touch any of us today. Do not think that the enemy can come against you without God's permission. It is impossible, especially now that God lives inside us.

The reality is, the enemy has no power or right to us any longer. A border of protection has been formed around us. There are angels encamping around us at this very moment. Even if you are a Christian struggling with some aspect of your flesh, know that you belong to God. Go to Him for forgiveness as many times as necessary and your covering will remain. The enemy wants you to step outside of God's presence so he can attack you at will, but if you stay in Christ, declare that...

Today's Declaration:

I AM PROTECTED FROM THE EVIL ONE

Day 56

I AM SECURE IN CHRIST

I give them eternal life, and they shall never perish; no one will snatch them out of my hand. My Father, who has given them to me, is greater than all; no one can snatch them out of my Father's hand.
John 10:28-29

We live behind bars, padlocks, and security systems. Our cars are governed by security systems so advanced, we can end up locked out of our cars, or stranded by the side of the road. It is amazing that we can have greater peace of mind with man-made security. Where is the peace of mind we should have from the God of the universe living inside us?

Security has become one of our top priorities in this day and age. We hesitate to leave our doors and windows open if we are not home. Yes, we need to be careful and take steps to prevent loss, but while we protect what we own, can we also protect ourselves? Some individuals opt to get themselves a firearm. Then thieves who come, run the risk of losing their lives in the process, but those thieves will also come for your gun if they knew you have one. The ends may not justify the means.

All the security in this world means nothing if we are not secured in Christ. Why are so many famous people, who can afford all the luxuries of life, including maximum security, killing themselves? What prevents them from wanting to live until their appointed time? These are the questions people are afraid to answer. For us, who know better, be confident and walk in the assurance that God has our backs.

Today's Declaration:

I AM SECURE IN CHRIST

Day 57

I AM SET ON A ROCK

He lifted me out of the slimy pit, out of the mud and mire;
he set my feet on a rock and gave me a firm place to stand.
Psalm 40:2

Jesus delved deep into the mind of Peter to find his thoughts. Peter declared that Jesus was "the Christ, Son of the living God." Jesus affirmed that on that rock (understanding and revelation) He would build His church, and hell could not prevail against it.

Sin is a sinking hole. Those who have walked in the deeper parts of this pit know that eventually we become covered and stuck beyond our control.

At 14, I was masturbating. At 18, I was deeply addicted to porn. At 24, I was fornicating, masturbating, and hooked on porn. We tend to sink deeper and deeper into sin. No sin travels alone. Every liar is a potential thief. Every porn abuser is a potential rapist. There is no end to sin, and no satisfaction.

Jesus pulled us out of that when we choose to follow Him in obedience. He placed our feet on a rock. The church is built on a rock, and we are the church. Even when we choose to crouch and dip our fingers in the muddy pool surrounding us, we are no longer under the power of sin. We are no longer sinking.

Today's Declaration:

I AM SET ON A ROCK

Day 58

I AM MORE THAN A CONQUEROR

No, in all these things we are more than conquerors through him who loved us.
Romans 8:37

This is one of my personal declarations. First, we must understand what it means to be more than a conqueror.

As Christians, we are not promised a life free of trials and tribulations. We are promised comfort in trying times, help in tough times, and deliverance from our troubles. The truth is, trials and tribulations are necessary to build faith and character. Each test that we go through makes us stronger.

That is why we find ourselves going through different levels of testing. Porn may be a thorn in our flesh for a season – or in my case, for years. When God finally delivered me from this addiction, He also taught me how to stay delivered. I did not just conquer this addiction; I learned how to keep conquering it. That is what it means to be more than a conqueror. We fall, but we learn to get up and keep moving. It is God's design, and it is perfect.

If a rock is beaten constantly by a hammer, eventually it is shattered. We are different. We are God's ultimate design and He fashioned us in such a way that the more we are hammered, the less likely we are to break.

When Paul finally understood this, he declared that he would glory in persecution and hardships as God's strength is made perfect in his weakness. Paul was practically saying, "Send more trouble." The more difficulty we face, the more God's glory will be manifested in our life.

So, speak to your circumstances and difficulties and let them know that…

Today's Declaration:

I AM MORE THAN A CONQUEROR

Day 59

I AM BORN AGAIN

For you have been born again, not of perishable seed, but
of imperishable, through the living and enduring word of
God.
1 Peter 1:23

To be born again requires a putting off of the old and assuming the new. It is to be integrated into a new culture; a re-socialization of sorts. Nicodemus once asked Jesus what it required to be saved. He heard these words, and was confused. How can a man enter again into his mother's womb? But Jesus was not talking about a natural birth. He was referring to a spiritual birth.

Because of sin, there is a need for man to be reborn. The way has been made, the method has been established, the means has been made known, and the possibility realized in the person of Jesus Christ. If there was no Jesus, there could be no born-again experience. If He is the way, then obeying the steps He outlined is the necessary process of being born again.

Whoever believes and is baptized will be saved, but
whoever does not believe will be condemned.
Mark 16:16

138

Take note of two steps outlined here by Jesus. He said that we first believe, then get baptized, and we will be saved.

We still teach as a church that it is enough just to believe and say a sinner's prayer. There are other verses of scripture that suggest that this is enough, but we are never to interpret the Bible in isolation. It is wrong of us to delay someone's baptism, as it is a part of the process of being born again.

Acts 2:38 - Peter replied, "Repent and be baptized, every one of you, in the name of Jesus Christ for the forgiveness of your sins. And you will receive the gift of the Holy Spirit."

In essence, to be born again is to be buried with Christ (immersion) and resurrected with Him to a new life. The old has passed, and all things have become new.

Today's Declaration:

I AM BORN AGAIN

Day 60

I AM A VICTOR

For everyone born of God overcomes the world. This is the
victory that has overcome the world, even our faith.
1 John 5:4

D o you want to hear some awesome news? Our position
as victors in Christ was established, decided, and came
into effect over 2,000 years ago. Two thousand years ago,
nobody knew you would be here. In another 100 years, your
children would have assumed this position depending on the legacy
you leave behind, as you would have probably moved on to glory.
It is incredible that each generation can be born victors.

So, let us put things into perspective. Before you were born,
your sins were paid for in full. Before you were born, death and the
devil were defeated in public. Before you were born, Christ paid
the price for your health and prosperity. This is your inheritance, a
gift; you only need to accept. Assume your rightful place as a victor,
and let no voice tell you otherwise. This is your legacy. This is your
destiny.

Today's Declaration:

I AM A VICTOR

Day 61

I AM HEALED BY HIS STRIPES

*We all, like sheep, have gone astray, each of us has turned
to our own way; and the Lord has laid on him the iniquity
of us all.*
Isaiah 53:6

*But he was pierced for our transgressions, he was crushed
for our iniquities; the punishment that brought us peace
was on him, and by his wounds we are healed.*
Isaiah 53:5

*Who his own self bare our sins in his own body on the tree,
that we, being dead to sins, should live unto righteousness:
by whose stripes ye were healed.*
1 Peter 2:24 - KJV

I have seen numerous visual interpretations of the crucifixion of Christ. It is never easy to watch, and still no one has captured a full and proper interpretation of the event.

The Bible says that Jesus was marred beyond recognition. When He received those 39 lashes, His flesh was ripped from His body and face. He was supposed to get 40 lashes, so you can imagine His state when they stopped at 39 and spared Him that final lash. It is believed that there are 39 major diseases inflicting mankind today. I don't know if it is true or not, but it is an interesting thought. "By his stripes, we are healed." I am deeply burdened when I go to church and see the sick come in and go out still sick. At what point in the history of the church did we grow content with this being the norm? We should not be sick because Jesus already paid the price for our health. Every sickness that we face was nailed to the cross, and we need to be liberated from the thought that we will be sick.

Scripture is correct when it says people perish for lack of knowledge. I hear people pronounce sickness on themselves daily. They say things like, "I am sick," "I am suffering," "I am dying." Even if these appear to be a reality in our natural realm based on how we feel and the diagnoses we received from doctors, the reality in the real (spiritual) world is that there is no more sickness or death.

Here we are torn between two worlds: a natural world that says one thing, and we often agree, and a supernatural world that says something entirely different from our present reality. We need to decide now which is the real world and which carries more validity. If we limit our existence to the natural world, then Christ suffered and died in vain. In fact, He created a new reality for us that includes health and wealth. Though we do not see it, it is there. We need to speak it until that becomes our reality.

Faith is our connection to the real world. It teaches us to believe things that are not yet as if they are.

Today's Declaration:

I AM HEALED BY HIS STRIPES

Day 62

I AM COVERED BY THE BLOOD OF JESUS

They overcame him by the blood of the Lamb and by the
word of their testimony; they did not love their lives so
much as to shrink from death.
Revelation 12:11

For you know that it was not with perishable things such
as silver or gold that you were redeemed from the empty
way of life handed down to you from your ancestors, but
with the precious blood of Christ, a lamb without blemish
or defect.
1 Peter 1:18-19

There is power in the blood of Jesus. The struggle for us is that we cannot see this blood. Very often we feel embarrassed speaking this blood over our lives. Others look on and are tempted to pass judgment. We need to understand that this blood is precious and should not be used in ignorance and pride. It is the price God paid for our redemption.

Let us examine the cross. At the moment when Jesus' side was pierced, both blood and water flowed. Some believe that water came because there was no more blood. Jesus shed all His blood (one or two gallons) for humanity.

All the blood in Jesus body could have filled your body if you had no blood. This is a divine operation performed on a wooden cross: Jesus did a blood transfusion, replacing our blood with His own. It is pure and undefiled and carries with it all the power that heaven affords. We are privileged to be under this covering.

Today's Declaration:

I AM COVERED BY THE BLOOD OF JESUS

Day 63

I AM SHELTERED UNDER HIS WINGS

*He will cover you with his feathers, and under his wings
you will find refuge; his faithfulness will be your shield and
rampart.
Psalms 91:4*

Scripture has some amazing examples of just who our God is
to us, and what He does on our behalf. These are examples
pulled from the natural world that we see and know. One
such example is that of the eagle. This spectacular bird is used
several times in the Bible relating to God's care for us. Here, He
covers us with His feathers, and under His wings we find refuge.

The eagle is very protective of its young. Eagles will go to great
lengths to protect those who belong to them, even sacrificing their
life. God has already given His life for us. Now He shelters and
protects us, and He's consistently faithful in doing so. At no point
are we left exposed or defenceless.

Today's Declaration:

I AM SHELTERED UNDER HIS WINGS

Day 64

I AM HIDDEN IN THE SECRET PLACE OF THE ALMIGHTY

He who dwells in the shelter of the Most High will rest in
the shadow of the Almighty.
Psalms 91:1

King David's life is one of great interest. God considered him a man after His own heart, yet David could not build God's house because he had too much blood on his hands. David once slew 200 Philistines in battle; the enemy simply could not touch David. There is no record that at any point in battle was this great king wounded. We can understand how he was able to make such a statement about resting in the shadow of the Almighty.

In God, we are sheltered. In Christ, we have rest. The battle belongs to our God, so although it takes effort to obey and some level of action on our part, we don't fight our battles. To dwell in the shadow of the Almighty is to be almost invisible to the enemy. We are safe and secure under God. When the enemy sees us, they see God. This is the safest place for a child of God to be.

Today's Declaration:

I AM HIDDEN IN THE SECRET PLACE OF THE ALMIGHTY

Day 65

I AM WALKING IN DIVINE HEALTH

But he was pierced for our transgressions, he was crushed
for our iniquities; the punishment that brought us peace
was on him, and by his wounds we are healed.
Isaiah 53:5

In heaven, there is no sickness, pain or death. In the present time (now) we are citizens of heaven. If we fully understand this, then it makes sense to accept that we are already walking in divine health, even if our minds and bodies say otherwise. I believe this is one of the most vital and important positions in Christ that the church needs to embrace.

There are signs, miracles, and healings taking place in various parts of the world. In Jamaica, we seem to have grown content with nothing happening. It burdens me when the sick come to church and go home sick; when the handicapped, blind, and deaf come to church and go back the same way. What, then, is the purpose of church, if we consistently fail to do what the church is meant to be doing?

We have lost sight of what is important, and our priorities are twisted. We pay so much attention to activities, physical structures, and time management that we limit the movement of the Holy Spirit. We do not even want to lay hands on anyone, and we find a scripture to support our hesitation. The result is that members of the church are dying from cancer, pneumonia, and heart attacks. Why?

If there are 39 main infirmities that attack our bodies, then each of those was placed on the body of Christ. He has already paid the price for our health. As I write this, I thank God for a full restoration of my mind and body. I have a fungus on my skin that itches, I am losing hair on the top of my head, I have two bad knees that make it hard to sit and get up, and I have anxiety issues. Yet, and despite all, I declare that I am walking in excellent health.

I have walked in the natural all my life, but all we see and know is just a shadow of the real world. In the real world, I am healthy and whole. I am in the same health as Jesus Christ, and the natural reality will have to bow its knees to the supernatural actuality. If I speak sickness and death, I nullify the complete work of Christ. Jesus declared, "It is finished." The work is done! I am healed.

Today's Declaration:

I AM WALKING IN DIVINE HEALTH

Day 66

I AM WALKING IN DIVINE WEALTH

For you know the grace of our Lord Jesus Christ, that
though he was rich, yet for your sake he became poor, so
that you through his poverty might become rich.
2 Corinthians 8:9

I believe that entrepreneurship was a part of God's original design for man, especially those who are called by His name. We are meant to be the head and not the tail; to be above and never beneath. Christians should be the ones creating jobs and leading corporations, companies, franchises, and local businesses.

Very often it is fear that stops us from achieving. We are afraid to fail, so the world has taken the initiative and moved into these unoccupied areas. So, we have to work for them, and help them achieve their dreams, while ours creep steadily to the grave where they will rest for all eternity.

Where are the Mark Zuckerbergs in the church? Where are the Bill Gates and the Carlos Slim Helús? Every successful business started with a dream and was built on persistence through difficulties and failures. Our problem is that we want the final product, but we want to skip the process.

Every believer can create wealth, with no exceptions. Yes, you have the capacity to create wealth. Christ died to make sure of it and it is who we are in Him. We have embedded within us great and supernatural wealth.

I never saw myself writing plays, movies, or books. When I started, I was not very good at it. It took over two years before I made my first sale, and I have been selling ever since. I have not amassed any great wealth yet, but all the pieces are in place, and I could achieve this milestone any day now by the mercy and grace of God.

Whatever is inside you needs to come out. You start by speaking it. Eventually, you will begin to believe it and live it. The world that you see is not the real world. This natural world came out of the real world, which is spiritual and supernatural. In the real world, you are wealthy. Declare it and believe it until it becomes your reality.

Today's Declaration:

I AM WALKING IN DIVINE WEALTH

Day 67

I AM HIS ANOINTED

The Spirit of the Lord is on me, because he has anointed
me to proclaim good news to the poor. He has sent me to
proclaim freedom for the prisoners and recovery of sight for
the blind, to set the oppressed free, to proclaim the year of
the Lord's favor.
Luke 4:18-19

We have a great responsibility in this world that most Christians fail to live up to. It is the reason God poured His Spirit out on us. We have been anointed and appointed for such a time as this.

So here is a truth, a revelation for the now generation: we should not encounter the poor, and not proclaim the good news to them. We should not encounter prisoners and not proclaim freedom. We should not encounter a blind person and not lay hands on them and declare them healed, even if it doesn't happen. We should make every attempt to free the oppressed and proclaim the gospel of the Kingdom of God.

We are wrong to look at a blind person and have only compassion. Compassion is good, but it should compel us to love. Love is produced when we act on compassion.

I understand our fear of praying and ministering to someone in need with no results, but it does not negate our responsibility to do it. How can we say we are anointed if we do not do what that anointing compels us to do? I am sure that even as you read this, your mind will locate some instance in the past where you were compelled to do something for someone in need, and you chose not to.

Every opportunity we get to act on our anointing should be pursued!

Today's Declaration:

I AM HIS ANOINTED

Day 68

I HAVE ACCESS TO THE FATHER

*Therefore, since we have been justified through faith, we
have peace with God through our Lord Jesus Christ,
through whom we have gained access by faith into this grace
in which we now stand. And we boast in the hope of the
glory of God.*
Romans 5:1-2

In times past, access to the Father was only granted to a
Levitical priest who was holy, cleansed, and sinless. No one
else had access to what was known as the "holy of holies,"
where the presence of God sat on Earth.

God always wanted a more personal and intimate relationship
with you and me. He designed human reproduction in such a way
that each of us is born with different characteristics and
personalities. We think differently, reason differently, act
differently, talk differently, and relate differently. It was always
God's desire to enjoy this diversity and variety in a close
relationship. He had it once in the garden of Eden. He wanted to
have it again.

Jesus came and made it possible. God, in flesh, came and
restored what He had lost in the garden. On the day Jesus died,
God ripped the veil in the temple in two, signifying full access to
the Father for all human beings.

We are clothed in the righteousness of Jesus, so we can
approach the throne boldly. He has declared you sons and

daughters of the most high God. We are no longer servants, but children of God.

Sadly, most of us still approach God as servants who are not worthy to come to Him. The Father is not pleased with this kind of mindset. A friend of mine will tell you that angels have to stand in God's presence, but the Word tells us we are seated with Christ in heavenly places.

If you have an excellent relationship with your earthly father, then you have a good idea of the kind of relationship God wants to have with you. Rejoice as you make this declaration to the spirit of timidity, inferiority, condemnation, unworthiness, fear, and guilt...

Today's Declaration:

I HAVE ACCESS TO THE FATHER

Day 69

I HAVE A HOME IN HEAVEN

Do not let your hearts be troubled. You believe in God;
believe also in me. My Father's house has many rooms; if
that were not so, would I have told you that I am going
there to prepare a place for you?
John 14:1-2

Paul said that if in this life alone we had hope, we would be most miserable. Throughout the ages, this has rung true for everyone who has been touched by grief. It is a road we walk in this life if we live long enough. I struggled after the death of my father, but the Holy Spirit spoke to me. He said, "If I must live, I will have to learn to deal with death." This is the point where I stopped hiding from death.

Heaven is our real home. Our final home will be on a New Earth and Heaven (Revelation 21:1). This is the hope of all those who put their trust in God. Jesus has changed our destiny to an eternity reigning with Him. He said all that belongs to Him belongs to us.

Imagine that great city built by His hands. He spoke these words nearly two thousand years ago, and it is possible that the city is not yet completed. Every precious stone that is shaped and laid is an act of His love towards us. His desire is for us to be where he is.

Today's Declaration:

I HAVE A HOME IN HEAVEN

Day 70

I HAVE ALL THINGS IN CHRIST

Therefore let no one boast in men. For all things are yours.
(1 Corinthians 3:21 - NKJV).

This revelation took my breath away. Faith took on a whole new meaning for me. It is not enough to believe that God exists, or that His Son walked this Earth. The Bible says that even demons believe and tremble. If we are to walk in the fullness of the power of the Kingdom, we have to believe in who we become in Christ.

The Bible says all that He has belongs to us. We are co-heirs of the Kingdom with Jesus Christ. We must develop faith in who we truly are in Christ, and have the confidence that whatever we ask the Father for, we have already received it because He takes pleasure in giving us what we ask Him for. That is who we are in Christ.

We can believe God but doubt He will do anything for us – it is the unworthiness complex we walk around with after coming into Christ. We are clothed in the righteousness of God, but we keep casting the garment aside for our old clothes and walk in doubt, guilt, and condemnation. As a result, we receive very little or nothing at all.

It is impossible to please God without faith, and not just faith in His existence, but faith in all He says we are. If we doubt His Word about us, we call Him a liar. But God cannot lie.

In Christ, we have all things. Whatever we want, we can ask Him for it and thank Him for it. God is a giver. He loves and takes pleasure in giving good gifts. We lack because we keep refusing His gifts. The good news is that faith comes by hearing and hearing the Word of God. This is God's Word, so speak it until you begin to believe it…

Today's Declaration:

I HAVE ALL THINGS IN CHRIST

Day 71

I HAVE A LIVING HOPE

Praise be to the God and Father of our Lord Jesus Christ!
In his great mercy he has given us new birth into a living
hope through the resurrection of Jesus Christ from the dead.
1 Peter 1:3

Hope is connected to faith. A more recent definition I read of faith is that "faith is not what you see, but what you hope for." King David went through many troubles and trials and proved God through them all. He said that God would "deliver us from them all." He went into many battles and saw himself walking away unharmed. He felt depressed at one point and spoke to his soul, commanding it to "hope in God."

What would life be if there was no God? Paul gave this question deep consideration and came to the following conclusion, "If only for this life we have hope in Christ, we are of all people most to be pitied" (1 Corinthians 15:19). I think that sums it up nicely. Christ is our living hope: the thought of a better tomorrow free from death, sin, tears, demons, sickness, and pain.

No matter what we are going through today, we should never lose hope in God. His promises sustain us through difficult periods, and we know that in Christ there is upward mobility.

He never leaves us in one position but pulls us through various seasons that strengthen and solidify our faith. We often look back and see a clearer picture of what God was doing through some of our most doubtful experiences. It is easy to see the whole valley once we get to the top of the mountain, but we must learn that in the valley we must keep our eyes focused on the mountaintop. That is our hope and destination.

Today's Declaration:

I HAVE A LIVING HOPE

Day 72

I HAVE AN ANCHOR FOR MY SOUL

*We have this hope as an anchor for the soul, firm and
secure. It enters the inner sanctuary behind the curtain.*
Hebrews 6:19

Faith is the substance of things hoped for, and the evidence of things not seen. Hope believes in the invisible, and may be one of our primary connections to the supernatural.

Imagine someone with stage four cancer declaring that they are walking in divine health. This is not an easy feat, and most who are sick are unable to do so. It is amazing that we put our hope in doctors (created by God) and medicine (substances created by God; the knowledge and ability to put them together coming from God) rather than in the Almighty. I am not saying we should not go to the doctor, but why do we go to the doctor first? We are admonished to seek first the Kingdom of God for wealth, health, and all our needs. If God directs us to the doctor, then by all means we should walk in obedience to Him. Our error is when we put greater faith in everything else but God.

Our hope is unmoving and cannot be touched, modified, or affected by mortal man. The Bible uses strong words to describe our hope: it is an anchor. In the natural, an anchor keeps ships in place, regardless of their size and circumstances. No storm can move a ship that is anchored. If it is to be destroyed, it will have to be destroyed where it is anchored.

That is how powerful hope is. Despite your circumstances or location, remain rooted in the Lord, your God.

Today's Declaration:

I HAVE AN ANCHOR FOR MY SOUL

Day 73

I HAVE A HOPE THAT IS SURE AND STEADFAST

We have this hope as an anchor for the soul, firm and secure. It enters the inner sanctuary behind the curtain.
Hebrews 6:19

We were created to exist independently, to some extent. We can choose to live independently of God, even though we still need His breathe to be alive. If this were not the case, there could be no atheists. God wants us to serve Him by choice, not by force.

Our daily lives are composed of the decisions we make from day to day. Each choice has a consequence or a benefit. One such is hope. Hope is built into our existence, but the choice we are faced with is what to put our hope in. Depending on where we direct our hope, our lives will adjust accordingly.

The writer of Hebrews speaks of hope that acts as an anchor. I hear King David speaking life to his depressed soul. He commanded his soul to "hope in God." I think that is a firm source for our ability to hope.

Some put their hope in a better world, improved economy, increased salary, and change of government—but none of these things offer any lasting consolation. In God alone I put my trust.

Today's Declaration:

I HAVE A HOPE THAT IS SURE AND STEADFAST

Day 74

I HAVE AUTHORITY TO TREAD ON SERPENTS

*I have given you authority to trample on snakes and
scorpions and to overcome all the power of the enemy;
nothing will harm you.*
Luke 10:19

Moments after Adam and Eve sinned, God declared that the seed of a woman would bruise the head of the serpent. Amazingly, satan is often referred to as a serpent. So, when Jesus came, amid all the other prophecies He had to fulfil, He also trampled the serpent under His feet. He was the first man to do that, and He gave us the authority to go and do likewise. We have power over the serpent that caused the fall of humanity.

For most Christians, the enemy appears ultimately intimidating. After all, who wants to be around after hearing a lion roar? But the Scripture is very specific to say that satan is "like" a roaring lion. There is only one Lion of the tribe of Judah, and His name is Yeshua. The same authority He has, we have. Greater is He that is in us, than He that is in the world.

The devil is a deceiver, which means his weapon is talk. He drives fear into us with words, but there is a Word greater than his. Our main weakness is our neglect of the Word of God.

If we don't know who we are, there is no way we can do what we are equipped and authorized to do. This is why so many of us end up under the influence of satan. This should not be the case, but people perish for lack of knowledge.

The question is, now that you know, what are you going to do about it?

Today's Declaration:

I HAVE AUTHORITY TO TREAD ON SERPENTS

Day 75

I HAVE POWER TO WITNESS

*But you will receive power when the Holy Spirit comes on
you; and you will be my witnesses in Jerusalem, and in all
Judea and Samaria, and to the ends of the earth.*
Acts 1:8

Jesus once said that the harvest was ripe, but the laborers are few
and asked His disciples to pray to the Father to send more
laborers (See Matthew 9:37-38). In those days, there were maybe
120 disciples. Imagine that figure against the population of the
world. If Jesus is the only way, only those few knew it. They took
the good news (Gospel) and carried it to different parts of the
world, and through them the world was evangelized.

Today there are over 7 billion people on the planet. Of this
number, there are 648 million Evangelical Christians. During Jesus
time, there were between 300 and 500 million persons living on the
planet. I would like to think that the Father has sent more laborers
now, but how many Christians today are witnessing to non-
Christians?

There are some who believe that their lives will witness
without having to say a word. The whole purpose of this book is
to highlight the power of the spoken word. We have a responsibility
to live the gospel, but it also has to be spoken to non-Christians.
Otherwise, it has no power.

There are people in my family who are not yet saved, and some
who are backslidden. There are people I have been close to who

have died without Jesus. My burden is great as I never mentioned the gospel to such persons. They were not saved by my life and mannerisms only. I needed to tell them, to proclaim the good News, but I did not. How many do you know who have died without you mentioning the life-giving gospel of Jesus Christ?

I was taught growing up that the baptism of the Holy Spirit was "power for service." This suggests an ability to work in the church in different capacities.

Others are endowed with the Spirit of God and only speak in tongues. The power of the Holy Spirit gives boldness to witness. God's greatest desire is to save the lost, not maintain the church. The church is the body of Christ filled with His Spirit in this world. It is not a building, a group of auxiliaries, functions, and activities, but people who will carry His message to the lost. We missed the mark when we started to apply a structure to His church. We turned it into a program within the limits of time and consideration for those who do not want to be at church in the first place. Our top priority should be to proclaim God's Word to those who are not yet believers. That is what the body of Christ is doing today. If you are not, then you are not yet a working part of Christ's body. The Holy Spirit gives us the power to be witnesses.

Today's Declaration:

I HAVE POWER TO WITNESS

168

Day 76

I HAVE THE TONGUE OF THE LEARNED

The Sovereign Lord has given me a well-instructed tongue,
to know the word that sustains the weary. He wakens me
morning by morning, wakens my ear to listen like one
being instructed.
Isaiah 50:4

It is amazing, the power we have inside us. The very Word that created all things lives in us. The Holy Spirit of God lives in us. We really can do all things because God lives in us, enables us, empowers us, and equips us.

Peter did not have a degree in theology, but after he was baptized with the Holy Spirit, he awed those who heard him speak. Jesus was only 12 years old when He answered questions that perplexed the learned men. You are no different. You have no less access to the same Spirit than any of these examples from Scripture.

Have you ever entered into a situation unsure of what you would say? Have you ever had the experience of shocking yourself with the words coming out of your own mouth? Jesus once instructed His disciples that they should not worry about what they will say in any particular situation. When the time came, the right words would be given to them. Given to them by whom? Yes, the same Spirit who lives in you.

People look to us sometimes because they assume that we should possess a certain measure of wisdom as Christians. The truth is, we do. Nothing can catch our Father by surprise. He knows all things, and He has a Word for all things. Old folks usually say, "Open your mouth and God will fill it with words." We can modify that a bit. Whenever you open your mouth to speak, remember that you have the wisdom and knowledge of heaven as your primary source.

Today's Declaration:

I HAVE THE TONGUE OF THE LEARNED

Day 77

I HAVE THE MIND OF CHRIST

For, "Who has known the mind of the Lord so as to
instruct him?" But we have the mind of Christ.
1 Corinthians 2:16

The importance of speaking this over our lives cannot be over-emphasized. It is reported that one out of every four persons has a mental disorder. Some are mild, others more serious. So, use your imagination to identify three people you know. One out of those three probably has a mental disorder. If all three are normal, then you are the crazy one!

This is serious. Philippians 2 admonishes us to "have the same mindset as Christ Jesus." Understand that the war that is going on in the spiritual realm around us is centered around our minds. Whoever controls the mind controls you. God wants full control of us, as this is the only way for us to be free and to live to our full potential as human beings. It was the original design.

If we possess the mind of Christ, we possess heaven and the Kingdom of God. This is not a future state of being but can be a present reality. The Kingdom of God is inside every believer. Sadly, for most, it lies dormant because the fullness of the Kingdom is measured and determined by the state of our minds and the level of our faith.

In other words, we need to think right. It does matter what you feed your mind. Young people will struggle with sex and lust if all they listen to are love songs. The music industry has brainwashed us to think that all there is to life is money, sex and violence.

Hear what the Word says: "Whatever is true, whatever is noble, whatever is right, whatever is pure, whatever is lovely, whatever is admirable—if anything is excellent or praiseworthy—think about such things" (Philippians 4:8).

Do you want to experience a real transformation in your life? Learn to think your thoughts after God. It is possible and highly beneficial. Lay your hand daily on your forehead and boldly declare...

Today's Declaration:

I HAVE THE MIND OF CHRIST

Day 78

I HAVE BOLDNESS AND ACCESS

Therefore, brothers, since we have confidence to enter the
Most Holy Place by the blood of Jesus.
Hebrews 10:19

When God looks at us, He sees the blood of Jesus. We are clothed in the righteousness of God. I cannot say that enough. It is a critical revelation that we need to receive to have the kind of relationship God desires with us.

In times past, very few had access to God's throne. Now we have access to the very holy of holies. This was once a place reserved for those who had absolutely no sin. How is it possible that we now have access? Jesus Christ made it possible. So when we come to God, it should be in reverence and respect, but not in fear and unworthiness. If we were unworthy, we could not approach God. If what Jesus had done did not take care of all our sins, we could not kneel by our bed and go to God. We could not stand in a church and go to God. The way has been made for us, and access given to all sons and daughters of God.

Let me say this in a different way. The same way God looks at Jesus and regards Him as His perfect Son is the way He looks at us. This is only possible because of what Jesus did. He took our place, so our sin is no longer relevant.

Don't get me wrong – we should not sin, and when we do, we should genuinely repent. But our sin no longer banishes us from the presence of God. We can go before God and repent because

Jesus' blood covers us. This is the confidence we have, and we should demonstrate as we come into God's presence. God does not condemn us. The enemy condemns us and seeks to pluck us out of God's presence. Stay in God's presence, even if you sin.

There was a point in my Christian life when I was sinning every day. I had to ask for forgiveness every single night, sometimes more than once a day. I lived like this for years. The consequences of my sin were great, but I never left the presence of God and He honoured my choice by delivering me from my self. Even if you have lost your way, or are addicted to some sin, clothe yourself in Christ and go to your Father. He eagerly waits for you.

Today's Declaration:

I HAVE BOLDNESS AND ACCESS

Day 79

I HAVE PEACE WITH GOD

Therefore, since we have been justified through faith, we
have peace with God through our Lord Jesus Christ.
Romans 5:1

There is a peace that surpasses understanding. This peace keeps us calm in the midst of tragedy. This peace confirms God's Word in our lives when we ask Him about the choices we need to make. This peace helped me to know that I was getting married to the right woman. This peace causes us to sleep at night even when there is a storm raging in our lives. This peace will clothe us with happiness in the midst of depression and anxiety. This peace puts a smile on our face when we are about to depart from this world.

This is a precious gift from God and one we should readily accept. We do have a natural ability to cope with stress and changes in life… but many people crack under the pressure. What separates a child of God from a non-Christian is this peace that no man can adequately explain.

In a workplace, several employees are about to be laid off, including one Christian. No one can understand how this Christian can be so cool, calm, and happy in the midst of such crises, but the born-again Christian knows that no matter what, God will take care of him.

Confidence accompanies this peace we receive from God. The world cannot give it, and the world cannot take it away… but if you have it, they will come to you because they too want to experience this peace.

Today's Declaration:

I HAVE PEACE WITH GOD

Day 80

I HAVE FAITH LIKE A MUSTARD SEED

He replied, "If you have faith as small as a mustard seed,
you can say to this mulberry tree, 'Be uprooted and planted
in the sea,' and it will obey you."
Luke 17:6

A grain of mustard seed is a little smaller than a grain of rice. That is all we need to move our mountains, but I have learned the reason our mountains remain unmoved. It is not an absence of faith, but the presence of unbelief. We can have both at the same time.

How often have we said, "I know God can do it, but…?" Faith simply says, "I know God can do it." Doubt will always respond, "But He may choose not to." Doubt stops faith in its tracks.

Jesus said if we can remove doubt, then we can tell the mountain to move, and it will be moved. This is how we were created. Like God, we can speak things into being because we are made in His likeness and image. Yes, we sinned, but Christ has restored us through His death and resurrection.

This lesson of mustard seed faith was given when Jesus spoke to a fig tree, and it dried up from the roots. He then told us that we can do the same thing if we simply have faith.

So, we struggle from day to day with the presence of unbelief in our lives. Mountains are before us, Pharaoh's army behind us… we stand on the shores of the Red Sea with nowhere to turn. We stand on the banks of the River Jordon dreaming that we will somehow get to the other side, and we sit in boats torn by angry winds as we silently accept whatever life throws at us. We may even wonder why God will not deliver us. God is waiting for you to speak to the rock, hit the River Jordan with your mantle, or stretch out the staff in your hands by faith, and then watch God accomplish the very words that you spoke.

Faith says things that are not as if they are. In my present state of financial difficulties, God promises me prosperity, and I speak it over my life every day. Our lives will never change until we change what we say. Let faith do the talking and seal the lips of doubt and unbelief.

Today's Declaration:

I HAVE FAITH LIKE A MUSTARD SEED

Day 81

I CAN DO ALL THINGS THROUGH CHRIST

I can do all this through him who gives me strength.
Philippians 4:13

The economy is tough, and the statistics are alarming. Only three out of every 10 students who graduate from the university will get a job. We are forced to ask, "What about the other seven?" Very good question!

Lecturers are now telling students that they need to approach their careers with aggression and creativity. Instead of searching for jobs, they must create jobs. Entrepreneurship is the order of the day, yet there are still thousands, or millions, who sit at home unable to find their true passion and calling in the marketplace. Who would think I would be an international Christian playwright, screenwriter, and author? The odds were against me, but I knew there was something in me called success. These words reverberated in my innermost being: "I can do all things through Christ." Yes, there were dark days, troublesome, and trying days, and believing this one fact required persistence.

I never stopped moving forward, even when it felt like I was going nowhere.

So here is the truth, according to God's Word: the only limitations we have are those we put on ourselves. Again, we call God a liar if we say there are things we cannot do. That kind of thinking is contrary to who you are in Christ. There are millions of writers trying to make a living from their craft and failing miserably.

I did it because I believed I could and never stopped trying, and the best is yet to come. I took courses, made friends with like-minded people, prayed, sought the Lord's help, fasted, and persevered through the dark times while always reminding myself audibly that I can do all things through Christ! I never stopped trying.

Now that you have said it, remove the limitations and go for it. Know that the Father despises lazy people, so put your hand to work and He will bless your efforts a hundredfold. He promises that in Him, everything we touch will prosper. Claim it, speak it, and go do it!

Today's Declaration:

I CAN DO ALL THINGS THROUGH CHRIST

Day 82

I FIND MERCY AND GRACE TO HELP ME

*Let us then approach God's throne of grace with
confidence, so that we may receive mercy and find grace to
help us in our time of need.*
Hebrews 4:16

We have no control over some of the circumstances we face in life. It is inevitable that difficult times will come. It is through this that we develop character and faith. We may wish we could bypass the process sometimes, but God knows we need a thorn in the flesh from time to time.

The good news is that we are never allowed more than we can bear. I have looked at other lives and wondered how they make it through. There are parents who have to bury their children, terminal illnesses wreaking havoc in households, and increasing cases of mental illness. But there is an abundance of mercy and grace available to us at all times. We draw strength from this infinite supply in our times of need.

The Word tells us that where sin abounds, even more grace abounds. The more we experience, the greater the measure of mercy and grace available to us.

Today's Declaration:

I FIND MERCY AND GRACE TO HELP ME

Day 83

I COME BOLDLY TO THE THRONE OF GRACE

Let us then approach God's throne of grace with
confidence, so that we may receive mercy and find grace to
help us in our time of need.
Hebrews 4:16

There is a certain level of trust required on our part as we approach God's throne. Yes, the reverence and awe should be there, but know that we have a right to stand in God's presence because of Jesus. Adam and Eve had the distinct pleasure of having God come down in the cool of the day or they were able to go up to fellowship. This was the defining experience in their relationship with God. We lost that to sin, and our dominion on earth and rights as sons and daughters of God were taken from us.

Jesus restored us. We are like the first man, Adam, and God desires to have that close and intimate relationship with us. Too many of us walk to the throne of grace in condemnation, guilt, and shame. This is not what God expects of us. We would not approach our earthly father like that. If we could at least regard the Lord as we do our human fathers, then our relationship with Him would improve.

When you approach the Father in prayer, consider yourself first as a son or daughter. Know that you have every right to approach His throne. See yourself clothed in the righteousness of Jesus Christ, and boldly talk to your Father about everything. He loves to hear your voice. He admires our confidence in speaking with Him, and He will honor our obedience in approaching His throne boldly.

Today's Declaration:

I COME BOLDLY TO THE THRONE OF GRACE

Day 84

I QUENCH THE FLAMING ARROWS

In addition to all this, take up the shield of faith, with
which you can extinguish all the flaming arrows of the evil
one.
Ephesians 6:16

Some words spoken against you can set the whole course of your life on fire, but God has given us protection from these words with the Shield of Faith.

Who are you in Christ? The strength of your shield will be determined by how well you can answer that question. Understand that words cannot be distinguished with thoughts. We sometimes try to cancel a negative word in thought only, and seal our lips, but the shield will only work if you use it—in this case, speak it.

When I was growing up, my father's response to a bad report card was always the same: I would amount to nothing, and my life would be full of suffering. I struggled with this for years, as they lodged in my soul like arrows and the area became infected. As I grew in the knowledge of God and His Word, I came to realize that I had the power to quench all these fiery arrows. I was led by the Spirit to pull these darts, swords, and spears out of my soul, and I have been free ever since. Subsequently God has elevated me from failure to success.

Let us examine this shield even further. Paul used Roman culture on occasion to make his points. In this case, he referred to the Roman armor. A Roman soldier's shield was long and wide enough to cover the entire body. Nothing would get through. I hear David say, "You will not fear the terror of night, nor the arrow that flies by day, nor the pestilence that stalks in the darkness, nor the plague that destroys at midday. A thousand may fall at your side, ten thousand at your right hand, but it will not come near you." (Psalms 91:5-7). David was supernaturally shielded from all attacks of the enemy.

Fear not, soldier of Christ. You are shielded from all fiery darts by the very shield provided to you by God the Father. This protection is called, "faith."

Today's Declaration:

I QUENCH THE FLAMING ARROWS

Day 85

I TREAD ON SERPENTS

*I have given you authority to trample on snakes and
scorpions and to overcome all the power of the enemy;
nothing will harm you.*
Luke 10:19

These were the words of Jesus. His Words give life. He is the Word by which all things were created and is held together. So, if He gives you authority, what stops you from using it?

Too many Christians live in fear of the devil, but his bark is worse than his bite. As a matter of fact, he mostly barks. I must admit that he is very influential and convincing, but how much more powerful is the God that we serve? If God lives in us, why fear. We have the authority to overcome all the power of the enemy. The Word doesn't deny that the enemy has power but emphasizes that we have greater power.

The serpent and scorpions will come at us. They come to steal, kill, and destroy, and if we choose to cower in fear, we will be overcome. It is for us to stand in the authority given to us by Jesus.

Today's Declaration:

I TREAD ON SERPENTS

Day 86

I PROCLAIM FREEDOM TO CAPTIVES

The Spirit of the Sovereign Lord is on me, because the Lord has anointed me to preach good news to the poor. He has sent me to bind up the brokenhearted, to proclaim freedom for the captives and release from darkness for the prisoners.
Isaiah 61:1

If no one proclaimed this freedom over our lives, we would still be captives to sin. Because we have received this freedom, we have a responsibility to free others. As Christians, we cannot cross to the other side of the street when a non-Christian comes our way. We have friends and family who are not yet saved, and we laugh at the same jokes but hesitate to share the gospel with them. They do not need to see that you are just as human as they are—they need to hear that they are lost and need to be saved.

We pass so many captives throughout our days, but how many do we help? When was the last time you were a miracle to someone? Everyone needs a miracle.

As Christ body, we have a great responsibility to minister to the needs of others. In Jamaica, there are many young men on the streets wiping people's car windows for small change. We give them what we do not want, or what has little or no value to us. There are many on the streets who are hungry, and we do not stop to feed them; so many in need of clothes, and we fail to clothe them. Have you ever visited the hospital and ministered to those who are sick or even prayed for their recovery?

Our mandate is great. These are the fruits we are encouraged to bear. We should show love to everyone we encounter. No one comes to you by accident, and we are cautioned to entertain strangers, for we may just be entertaining angels.

Jesus took time out for everyone. We should do likewise. We have the message and words of freedom. It has no value if it is not demonstrated, and every day brings new and different opportunities.

If you need a miracle today, then be a miracle to someone else. What you make happen for others will come to pass for you.

Today's Declaration:

I PROCLAIM FREEDOM TO CAPTIVES

Day 87

I PRAY ALWAYS AND EVERYWHERE

Be always on the watch, and pray that you may be able to
escape all that is about to happen, and that you may be
able to stand before the Son of Man.
Luke 21:36

My greatest struggle as a child of God has always been with prayer. There were days when I would go to church and hide so I did not get called on to pray. (This is also one of the reasons for my most embarrassing moment at church, but that's water under the bridge.)

Prayer is key to a Christian's life. It is the greatest privilege we have as humans to come before a holy, eternal God and communicate with Him. There is no greater honor for a man, and there is nothing we struggle with more.

I remember needing some money to get through a very busy weekend. It was Saturday, and the banks were all closed, so my options were limited. God directed me to the Word, and I read where Jesus was in the garden of Gethsemane, on His knees in prayer. That was my answer: the Son of God praying on His knees. How much more should we do likewise? So, I went into my bedroom and closed the door. I got down on my knees and prayed the same prayer Jesus did. Ten minutes later I got a call about a check that was drawn on a bank that was open on Saturdays. God can do the impossible, but we need to pray.

We can come to the throne in prayer at any time of the day. However, I no longer believe this excuses us from reverence and proper posture in prayer. I think we approach God too casually, in all manner of attitudes and positions. Be mindful that you are praying to the God of the universe, and though we are His children, respect is due.

The Word admonishes us to replace worries and anxieties with prayer. We are to pray always, with supplication and thanksgiving, and never cease from praying. Jesus gave us the keys to the Kingdom. He told us that we would do greater things than Him. Most of us hold those keys and do not know how to use them.

Let us take an example from Jesus. He spent hours in prayer and took seconds to cast out demons and heal the sick. If we only spend minutes in prayer, how can we expect immediate results?

Prayer is the key to the Kingdom. We can lock and unlock, loose and bind. There is absolute power in prayer, not as a means in itself, but by pulling the realm of God into the earthly realm.

Finally, as you pray, learn also to listen.

Today's Declaration:

I PRAY ALWAYS AND EVERYWHERE

Day 88

I ROUT A THOUSAND

One of you routs a thousand, because the Lord your God
fights for you, just as he promised.
Joshua 23:10

With God, all things are possible. He takes odds that would naturally result in failure for us, and converts them into success. David once killed 200 Philistines and walked away from the battle unscathed. Gideon defeated a whole army with just 300 men. Joshua saw the impenetrable Jericho wall destroyed after following the Lord's instructions. The odds are never against us when we walk in obedience to the Word of God.

You may feel alone at times as if there is no one fighting by your side, but know that you can put 1,000 to flight, whether men or demons.

We were never meant to live and fight in isolation, but even Jesus was abandoned by His companions when He needed them the most. Peter disowned Him three times in succession. Jesus was alone, but not forsaken. He chose to walk that path so none of us would have to. So today, if you are faced with the same scenario, know that at least 1,000 will fall by your hands.

Today's Declaration:

I ROUT A THOUSAND

Day 89

I DEFEAT THE ENEMY

*They triumphed over him by the blood of the Lamb and by
the word of their testimony; they did not love their lives so
much as to shrink from death.*
Revelation 12:11

Jesus died to make us perpetual victors over the power of the
enemy. Satan stands defeated. We have a responsibility to
propagate that victory daily. Here we find two weapons that we
should use.

One is the blood of the Lamb that was poured out at Calvary.
The children of Israel put animal blood over the lintels of their
homes so that when the death angel walked through Egypt, he
passed by every home that was stained with blood. Jesus shed His
blood for the very same reason, except that His blood is on us. It
is through this covering we walk in victory every day.

The word of our testimony also has the power to defeat the
enemy. Too many people testify and exalt the enemy. Even if we
say he is trying to get us, he just loves to hear us calling his name.
Our testimony should be about God and what He has done in our
lives. I am reading a book on the supernatural. The more I read
other people's testimony of how God healed and delivered them,
the more my faith increases. That is the power of real testimony.

Do not be afraid to share your testimony with others. I was
not ashamed to admit my struggle with porn and masturbation.

That testimony has helped other young men who are presently struggling and seeking help to overcome it. We are encouraged to know that what we are going through has been experienced and overcome by others. These are just two of the ways we defeat the enemy.

Today's Declaration:

I DEFEAT THE ENEMY

Day 90

I TREAD SATAN UNDER MY FEET

The God of peace will soon crush Satan under your feet.
The grace of our Lord Jesus be with you.
Romans 16:20

Be encouraged that the schemes and efforts of the devil will not continue indefinitely. God is Alpha and Omega, Beginning and End, First and Last. We have a beginning, but in God we no longer have an end. The devil's end is coming, where he will no longer be allowed to co-exist with God's children.

We always sing in church that Satan is under our feet, and in a sense he is, but the ultimate crushing of his head is a future event. This is when God will crush the devil under our feet, heralding our final defeat of the kingdom of darkness.

Today's Declaration:

I TREAD SATAN UNDER MY FEET

Day 91

I CANNOT BE SEPARATED FROM GOD'S LOVE

Who shall separate us from the love of Christ? Shall trouble or hardship or persecution or famine or nakedness or danger or sword? As it is written: "For your sake we face death all day long; we are considered as sheep to be slaughtered." No, in all these things we are more than conquerors through him who loved us. For I am convinced that neither death nor life, neither angels nor demons, neither the present nor the future, nor any powers, neither height nor depth, nor anything else in all creation, will be able to separate us from the love of God that is in Christ Jesus our Lord.
Romans 8:35-39

David examined his life once and made the shocking observation that there was nowhere he could go that the presence of God would not be. We should view His wonderful love in this light.

What makes God's love so inseparable from us? He chose to love us while we were sinners. We had no thought or love towards Him, we did not regard Him, we did not esteem Him, but He chose to extend His love for us not just in words, but in action.

God's love is not merited, earned, or worked for. It is not a reward for loving God first. It is not something we can manipulate and exploit. God's love is universal, continuously persistent, and consistent. This is God's love, not ours. He has all power, and He loves us.

If that statement is true, and there is no higher power, then what could exist to pull us away from such love? Nothing!

Today's Declaration:

I CANNOT BE SEPARATED FROM GOD'S LOVE

Day 92

I CANNOT PERISH OR BE LOST

*I give them eternal life, and they shall never perish; no one
can snatch them out of my hand.*
John 10:28

*For God so loved the world that he gave his one and only
Son, that whoever believes in him shall not perish but have
eternal life.*
John 3:16

Jesus took our place. One author called it "a divine exchange."
Jesus had no sin, but He took all my sin. I had no righteousness,
but He gave me all His righteousness.

This is a significant part of human history that many struggle
with. I see so many people walk to the altar and are not ready to
accept Jesus. Some reject Christ with sophistication and dignity.
Others do not see how they need Jesus, or why so much
significance is placed on turning our lives over to Him.

These are people who are lost and will perish without Christ,
but they do not see that. Life seems significant enough without
God—as a matter of fact, God complicates things because when
we turn our lives over to Him, we do not get to do what we want.
The "playa" tries to do his own thing without God until he
contracts AIDS. The drunk lives life by his rules until he ends up
in court for a charge of manslaughter. The teenager goes down her
path until she discovers she is pregnant, and her whole life changes.

The criminal lives by his rules that eventually take him to prison or the grave.

There is no escaping the punishment of sin except through Jesus Christ. This is not about churches trying to make up their numbers or increase their weekly offerings. They are attempting to save lives, one soul at a time.

In Christ, we have eternal life. It was not earned, but given to us.

Today's Declaration:

I CANNOT PERISH OR BE LOST

Day 93

I CANNOT BE MOVED

I keep my eyes always on the Lord. With him at my right hand, I will not be shaken.
Psalms 16:8

We bear the image and likeness of our Creator. One trait we have adopted as sons and daughters of God is the ability to be immovable.

They will be like a tree planted by the water that sends out its roots by the stream. It does not fear when heat comes; its leaves are always green. It has no worries in a year of drought and never fails to bear fruit.
Jeremiah 17:8

To be in Christ suggests an ability to weather any storm. We are not affected by the climate, for even in drought and heat our leaves remain green. When other trees are not bearing fruit, our fruit remains. We are always producing, in season and out of season.

That person is like a tree planted by streams of water, which yields its fruit in season and whose leaf does not wither—whatever they do prospers.
Psalm 1:3

I was praying recently for some young people seeking jobs, and the Holy Spirit led me in another direction. We all have the gifting and ability to create wealth. Think about multi-millionaires who started franchises from the simplest thing: chicken, burgers, fish, etc. The Bible says whatever we do will prosper. So, I prayed instead that these persons would find the courage and initiative to create wealth. Wherever the Lord plants us, there we should produce and prosper.

Today's Declaration:

I CANNOT BE MOVED

Day 94

I CANNOT BE CHARGED OR ACCUSED

Who will bring any charge against those whom God has chosen? It is God who justifies.
Romans 8:33

We once stood accused in the court of eternity. Our sins were many—past, present, and future. We had no hope. The accuser took his place and reached for our file. Everything in it was true. We lied, stole, cheated, fornicated… and the list went on and on. We were powerless to save ourselves and knew that our punishment would be severe. The verdict came swift and hard. The final verdict was "guilty" and the sentence was death. There was no other way to punish sin.

But then God did something profound. He took our punishment in our stead. He died in our place.

Any human outside of Christ is dead. If we accept His sacrifice, we accept life. If we reject Him, we reject life. We are making a statement that we will pay for our own sins, and the penalty is death. There is no life outside of Christ, no matter what you think, feel, or believe. If Jesus had not died on that cross, all of us would stay dead. Now that we have accepted Christ, it is impossible for us ever to be charged or accused again.

It is easy to identify deception if we knew exactly who we are in Jesus Christ. The life that you think exists outside of Christ is a myth.

Today's Declaration:

I CANNOT BE CHARGED OR ACCUSED

Day 95

I CANNOT BE CONDEMNED

*Nevertheless, when we are judged in this way by the Lord,
we are being disciplined so that we will not be finally
condemned with the world.*
1 Corinthians 11:32

The world is condemned because of Adam's sin. We are all born into a world of sin; it is a part of our DNA.

Let us consider some substitute words for condemned: fated, destined, damned. When we are born again, we are released from this curse. We are no longer subject to the punishment that unbelievers will face at the end of this age. We will escape the coming judgment. We will give an account of our lives, but we will not be judged or condemned.

This is the freedom we have in Christ. He has fully liberated us from death and judgment. We walk out this freedom every day of our lives.

*Therefore, there is now no condemnation for those who are
in Christ Jesus.*
Romans 8:1

Friends, Jesus came that we might have life—and not just life, but abundant life. Christianity is not about church buildings, dress codes, rituals, traditions, activities, or religion. It is about restoring the kind of relationship that almighty God has always wanted to have with a unique set of people. He is intrigued by our different personalities and natural abilities, and He wants us to live an abundant and fulfilling life now and later. He paid the price—a gift that we cannot work for or will ever deserve. It is for us to receive this gift with thanksgiving.

We were sold into slavery to sin. God purchased us with His own blood. We are no longer condemned.

Today's Declaration:

I CANNOT BE CONDEMNED

Day 96

I AM THE VOICE OF GOD

*In a large house there are articles not only of gold and
silver, but also of wood and clay; some are for special
purposes and some for common use. Those who cleanse
themselves from the latter will be instruments for special
purposes, made holy, useful to the Master and prepared to
do any good work.*
2 Timothy 2:20-21

*Death and life are in the power of the tongue, and those
who love it will eat its fruit.*
Proverbs 18:21 - NKJV

Whatever God wants to say in this day and age is said through us. We are His voice in this world, but sometimes we silence God by not speaking.

Christ lives in us, ultimately manifesting Himself through us. It is unreasonable for us to expect God to speak independently of the temples that He occupies. Yes, all have access to the Word of God through the Bible, but unless there is a revelation, the Word will be read and not understood.

The apostle Phillip was told to go to a particular place where a eunuch was reading the scriptures. Of course, the eunuch did not understand what he read until Phillip explained it to him. Phillip revealed the meaning of the scriptures through the Holy Spirit. The eunuch immediately requested baptism.

We are God's voice in the world today. In all your years as a Christian, have you ever heard the audible voice of God? I supposed most of the answers will be no. We can understand why God would ask us to surrender our entire bodies to Him (See Romans 12:1). We are God's physical presence in this world right now. We are His hands, feet, heart, eyes, and voice in this Earth right now.

Today's Declaration:

I AM THE VOICE OF GOD

Day 97

I DIE DAILY

I face death every day—yes, just as surely as I boast about
you in Christ Jesus our Lord.
1 Corinthians 15:31

Then Jesus said to his disciples, "Whoever wants to be my
disciple must deny themselves and take up their cross and
follow me."
Matthew 16:24

I struggled for years to understand Jesus' instructions to deny self, take up the cross, and follow Him. It is already a challenge to simply do what Jesus did, but how do we deny ourselves? It must be possible if we are told to do it.

It was Paul who made the profound statement that he faced death every day, or as it is often translated, that he "died daily." He must have understood the command to be able to do it. When I finally got the revelation of self-denial, I realized that I was already doing just that.

Have you ever heard a Christian say they do only what they feel like doing? That is exactly what self-denial is not. To die daily means you no longer walk according to the dictates of the ego. You are not guided only by how you feel. No man can please God in the flesh; neither is the flesh interested in pleasing God.

To die daily means we no longer lean on our thoughts, emotions, and understanding, but put our trust in God. We are faced with the daily choice to either walk in the flesh or walk according to the Spirit.

The Father has been dealing with the unsurrendered areas of my life. I have surrendered my love for food, passivity, and silence. But I still had one area that was not submitted to God, and that was my sleep. I love to sleep, and God has unsuccessfully tried to wake me to pray on many occasions. Now that I am seeking his favor and supernatural manifestations in my life, He has pointed out that I am still not entirely surrendered. So, this is all I have left to give, and I am anxious to see what God will do in my life when I am fully surrendered.

In essence, I die so Christ has full freedom to live through me.

Today's Declaration:

I DIE DAILY

Day 98

I SPEAK THINGS INTO EXISTENCE

*The tongue has the power of life and death, and those who
love it will eat its fruit.*
Proverbs 18:21

*If you believe, you will receive whatever you ask for in
prayer.*
Matthew 21:22

This revelation changed my life.

We were created in the image and likeness of God. How did God create the natural world? He spoke it into being. Yes, the natural came out of the supernatural by the spoken word. This same Word now lives in us—the same Word that spoke all life as we know it into existence.

It matters what we say. The apostle James said that the tongue can set the whole course of your life on fire (See James 3:6). One of my good friends, Prophet David, mentioned that man is governed by the mind and mouth. These have the ability to enslave and to set one free. All our problems and issues can probably be traced back to something we said.

All things considered, we need to understand this unique and supernatural ability we have to speak things into being. If the same Spirit who moved upon the waters in Genesis now resides in our beings, why are we living so far below our potential?

Nothing is impossible for us through Christ. We are limited by our thinking and restricted by our words.

Over the centuries, some great and powerful concepts have been born from the mind of man. Take for instance the multi-billion-dollar social network, Facebook. We can cite many other examples of billion-dollar corporations built on simple ideas. These were produced in the minds of humans.

If all that can come from the mind of a man, imagine what can come from the mind of God. We need to start speaking from God's mind and not our own. The words we speak have the power to create and destroy.

Are you seeking a job? Create one. Do not piggyback on anyone's ideas or help others build their dreams. With God, there are no limits to what you can do. If you can speak it, it can be done.

Today's Declaration:

I SPEAK THINGS INTO EXISTENCE

Day 99

I AM EMPOWERED TO WALK IN THE SUPERNATURAL

*Believe me when I say that I am in the Father and the
Father is in me; or at least believe on the evidence of the
works themselves. Very truly I tell you, whoever believes in
me will do the works I have been doing, and they will do
even greater things than these, because I am going to the
Father.*
John 14:11-12

God's supernatural power inhabits every Christian, but
it requires a submitted and holy life to partake of it. The
working of that power, the fruit that is produced, is the
hallmark of a true disciple.

I grew up in a church culture that taught me not to expect
anything from God. My faith was never challenged deeply enough
to move or seek to go beyond the natural. I was taught that God is
God, and He does things according to His agenda. For instance, I
believed that tithes were supposed to be paid with no expectations
attached. These are just a few of the beliefs that blocked the flow
of the supernatural in my life. I believed I did not need the
manifestation of God's glory and power to be a child in the
Kingdom, and neither did the non-Christians. Apostle Paul
disagrees.

I was wrong! None of that is scriptural. The Bible is clear that the Kingdom of God is not talk, but power (See 1 Corinthians 4:20). Now I am deeply burdened as I have walked so long exclusively in the natural, without acknowledging that the natural world came out of the supernatural world. This suggests that the supernatural is dominant. In essence, the real world is that world we cannot see or interact with in a physical sense, though if God permits, we can encounter the spiritual in a physical sense. For instance, angels can be seen with the physical eyes.

Both worlds are run by laws. The natural is ruled by time, space, and matter. In the natural, we get sick, go to doctors and hospitals, take medicine, undergo operations, and ultimately die. In the supernatural there is no sickness or death. Faith is the link, the ability to see into and interact with the supernatural. Faith also causes a collision between both worlds. They collided after Lazarus lay dead in a tomb for four days. What Jesus did at that moment in time was demonstrate that the natural is dominated by the supernatural. If only we can grasp this revelation, the very atmosphere of the church will change.

In the supernatural, we are not sick. There is no cancer, AIDS, lupus, skin diseases, poverty, death, lack, or defeat. In the supernatural, all is perfect. Through Jesus Christ, the supernatural can become our present reality. That is what I am presently seeking the Lord for. Faith is now. The supernatural is now. And the natural is dominated by the supernatural.

The problem we face now is that most Christians do not seek after a supernatural experience in God. As a result, we witness to the lost with words and no power. Jesus demonstrated the power of the Kingdom and people believed. Throughout the book of Acts (concerning the early church), the disciples and apostles did the same thing. Today we mostly talk, but there is no demonstration of the very things we talk about. Very seldom do we see the Kingdom we talk about being manifested, and we have even created doctrines to support its absence.

The church needs to walk in the supernatural power of God. It was never God's plan for us to operate independently of His power. We should be showing people who God is, not just telling them. This is why people come but do not stay. We are making converts, but not disciples.

Rise up, child of God! The supernatural is real and can be a reality for us. This is what Jesus spoke about when He told us to "Seek first his kingdom and his righteousness" (Matthew 6:33). The Kingdom of God is a kingdom of power and authority. When we get sick, the doctor should not be our first thought. When we are broke, a bank loan should not be our first thought. Jesus taught us to pray, "Thy Kingdom come." That was the topic of a very powerful message preached by one of my pastors. God's kingdom applies to all areas of our lives; otherwise, all we have is religion. If we are not walking in the supernatural, we have a form of godliness, but deny its power (See 2 Timothy 3:5).

Today's Declaration:

I AM EMPOWERED TO WALK IN THE SUPERNATURAL

Day 100

I AM LOVE

*Dear friends, let us love one another, for love comes from
God. Everyone who loves has been born of God and knows
God. Whoever does not love does not know God, because
God is love. This is how God showed his love among us:
He sent his one and only Son into the world that we might
live through him. This is love: not that we loved God, but
that he loved us and sent his Son as an atoning sacrifice for
our sins. Dear friends, since God so loved us, we also ought
to love one another. No one has ever seen God; but if we
love one another, God lives in us and his love is made
complete in us.*
1 John 4:7-12

*For the Spirit God gave us does not make us timid, but
gives us power, love and self-discipline.*
2 Timothy 1:7

I wrote an article several years ago that was published in the
local newspaper titled, "What the World Needs Now is Love."
Nothing has changed.

Because of sin, it is not natural for us to love. It is easier to
covet, criticize, judge, and dislike. That is why born-again believers
must be given a spirit of power, love, and self-discipline. It takes
God for us to love, and God is love. Because God lives in us, we

become love. This new nature coexists with the old nature, so we are faced daily with the choice to walk in the flesh or walk in the Spirit. We should walk in the Spirit, and thus walk in love at all times. Eventually, we become what we do.

Those who encounter us should meet love. We often miss the precious opportunities that God provides for us daily. Understand that seldom does anyone cross our path accidentally or coincidentally. God wants to reach this world through us. He wants to love this world through us. We are God's demonstrated love to this world today, and there is no greater love that we can have than to be willing to lay down our lives for a friend. Do not value your life above another. In this way, the God of love is glorified. We are an embodiment of divine love.

Today's Declaration:

I AM LOVE

Day 101

I AM THE CHURCH

*Simon Peter answered, "You are the Messiah, the Son of
the living God." Jesus replied, "Blessed are you, Simon son
of Jonah, for this was not revealed to you by flesh and
blood, but by my Father in heaven. And I tell you that
you are Peter, and on this rock I will build my church, and
the gates of Hades will not overcome it.*
Matthew 16:16-18

*And God placed all things under his feet and appointed
him to be head over everything for the church, which is his
body, the fullness of him who fills everything in every way.*
Ephesians 1:22-23

The word "church" as rendered in the New Testament
comes from the Greek word Ekklesia, which is formed
from two Greek words meaning "an assembly" and "to call
out" or "called out ones." The New Testament Church is a body
of believers who have been called out from the world by God to
live as His people under the authority of Jesus Christ.

We are the church. Wherever we work, the church is there
because we are there. Wherever we go to school, the church is there
because we are there. Wherever we live, the church is there because
we are there. The presence of the church should be known and felt
in our particular geographical location. In essence, we do not invite

people to church; we should ask people to come and fellowship with the church.

We often give the impression that the church is only a sanctuary or building. This may have been the case under the old covenant, but the new one has come. We are still clinging to the shadow of what was, instead of embracing the new, and it hinders our influence on society.

When people come to you, they come to the church. When people come against you, they come against the church. There is an urgent need for us to understand this and get it right. God is not dwelling in your church building. He does not go there to wait for us to come to Him. He dwells in us and has sent us out into the world. You are the holy, sanctified place where God lives.

1 Corinthians 6:19-20 - Do you not know that your bodies are temples of the Holy Spirit, who is in you, whom you have received from God? You are not your own; you were bought at a price. Therefore honor God with your bodies.

The power of the church should be felt over the length and breadth of every nation in this world. You are like Christ on this Earth. He changed the world. You can change the world too.

Today's Declaration:

I AM THE CHURCH

APPENDIX

I am not who I feel like I am. I am not who I think I am. I am not who others think I am. I am who God says I am! Therefore, I will declare his truth about me every day:

- I am the head and not the tail. I am a victor, not a victim.
- I am strong and not weak. I am a saint, not a sinner.
- I am a child of God, not a child of the devil. I am free, not a slave to sin.
- I am clean, not dirty.
- I am above and not below.
- I am whole, not broken and bruised. I am rich, not poor.
- I am wise, not ignorant.
- I am adopted, not abandoned. I am kept by the power of God. I am able, not disabled.
- I am seated in heavenly places in Christ. I am an heir of God.
- I am a joint heir with Christ. I am more than a conqueror. I am a warrior, not a wimp.
- I can do all things through Christ who strengthens me.
- No evil can strike me, and no plague can come near my dwelling.
- I am safe and secure, kept in the palm of His hand.
- He who began a good work in me will perform it until the day Jesus comes again.
- I am the temple of God.
- I am indwelt and filled with the Holy Spirit.

- I am a vessel sanctified and ready for the Master's use.

I sincerely hope that you have found this devotional journey thought-provoking and helpful in your Christian journey.

If this devotional has helped you, please consider helping more people find it by leaving a review on Amazon.com or recommending it to others.

Shalom!

OTHER BOOKS BY AUTHOR C. ORVILLE MCLEISH

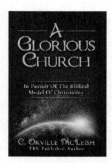
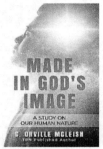

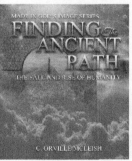

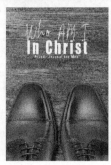

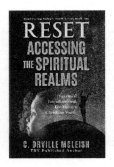
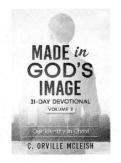

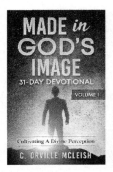
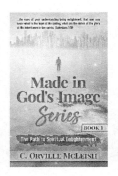

Printed in Great Britain
by Amazon

33713227R00126